KV-372-536

Contents

Volkswagen Beetle 1302S

What's in it for You?

Whether you've bought the book yourself, or had it given to you, the idea was probably the same in either case – to help you get the best out of your VW Beetle and perhaps to make your motoring a bit less of a drain on your hard-earned cash at the same time.

Garage labour charges can easily be several times your own hourly rate of pay, and usually form the main part of any servicing bill; we'll help you avoid them by carrying out the routine services yourself. Even if you *don't* want to do the regular servicing, and prefer to leave it to your VW dealer, there are some things you should check regularly just to make sure that your car's not a danger to you or anyone else on the road; we tell you what they are.

If you're about to start doing your own servicing (whether to cut costs or to be sure that it's done properly) we think you'll find the procedures described give an easy-to-follow introduction to what can be a very satisfying way of spending a few hours of your spare time.

We've included some tips that should save you some money when buying replacement parts and even while you're driving; there's a chapter on cleaning and renovating your car, and another on fitting accessories.

Apart from the things every Beetle owner needs to know to deal with mishaps like a puncture or a blown bulb, we've put together some Troubleshooter Charts to cover the more likely problems that can crop up with even the most carefully maintained car sooner or later.

There's also a set of conversion tables and a comprehensive alphabetical index to help you find your way round the book.

If the bug (or should it be Beetle?!) gets you, and you're keen to tackle some of the more advanced repair jobs on your car, then you'll need our Owner's Workshop Manual for the VW Beetle which gives a step-by-step guide to all the repair and overhaul tasks, with plenty of illustrations to make things even clearer.

Volkswagen Beetle 1303S

The Beetle Family

The VW Beetle was first introduced to the UK in 1952 with an 1131cc engine, but it was not until January 1954 that sales began in large numbers with the introduction of the 1192cc engine. Yearly model changes in the Beetle range were made on August 1st, but some changes were made half way through a production year. Because of this the only positive way to determine the year of a particular car is to check the chassis number with your local VW dealer, and the following information must only be used as a general guide.

The 1954 model had an 1192cc engine with an output of 30 bhp and was initially known as the Type 1. It was available as a standard or de luxe saloon. The starter motor switch was incorporated into the ignition switch and the rear window was round instead of the previous split type. The 1954 model body served as the basic body throughout the complete Beetle range.

1955 models were fitted with an uprated 34 bhp 1192cc engine and flashing indicators were fitted as standard.

The 1956 model incorporated a modified exhaust system with twin exhaust tailpipes. The front seat backrests were adjustable for rake and the steering wheel was modified with lower spokes. A 66 amp hour battery was fitted and the rear light clusters were raised 2 inches on the wings. Bumper overriders were fitted.

The 1957 model was fitted with tubeless tyres and the dash panel heater outlets were repositioned.

1958 models incorporated a larger windscreen and rear window, and because of the latter modification the engine cooling air intakes were lowered. Wider brake drums and linings were fitted on front and rear wheels, and the rear brake arrangement was changed through 180°. The front indicator lamps were repositioned on the top of the wings. The facia panel and accelerator pedal were modified.

The 1959 model incorporated a reinforced chassis and a modified fan belt and clutch springs. Radio interference suppression was incorporated late in the production year.

The 1960 model was fitted with modified seats and a front seat passenger footrest. A torsion bar was fitted to the front wheels and the steering wheel was fitted with a half-ring horn push. Exterior push buttons were fitted to the door handles, and a steering damper was incorporated late in the production year. A single rear lamp cluster was fitted and the generator output was increased.

1961 models incorporated an uprated 40 bhp engine with an increased compression ratio, and an all-synchromesh gearbox was fitted to de luxe models. A fully electric automatic choke was fitted to the carburettor, and the fuel tank was modified to give more room in the luggage compartment. The brake fluid reservoir was transparent for quick checking and a windscreen washer was fitted. The starter switch was modified to the 'non-repeat' type. Some major components of the engine (crankshaft, crankcase, cylinder head, valve gear etc) were redesigned.

The 1962 models incorporated a spring-loaded engine cover, enlarged rear light clusters, a modified heater outlet, compressed air windscreen washers, seat belt mountings, a fuel gauge, worm and roller steering, and a shorter gear lever, and the flasher indicator warning lamp was changed from red to green.

The 1963 models were fitted with leatherette headlining and the sunroof had a folding handle where fitted. The Wolfsburg bonnet crest was discontinued and the floor covering was foam insulated.

1964 models incorporated a horn thumb bar instead of the half-ring, improved seat covering, folding rear seat, new quarterlight and engine cover catches, and a new body colour range.

The 1965 model was designated the 1200A and **7**

was basically the same as the previous 1200, but the glass area was increased. The windscreen wipers, seats, braking system, heater, and engine cover catch were also slightly modified.

In August 1965 (ie 1966 model) the Beetle 1300 was introduced although the 1200A continued unchanged. The new model was an improved version of the 1200A and was fitted with a 1285 cc engine with an increased output of 50 bhp. In addition to the basic body version, the 1966 model was also available as a convertible, although imports of this model ceased in July 1966. Indicator and headlamp dip functions were incorporated in a single combination stalk.

1967 1200A models were fitted with additional trim including rubber floor mats, and a reserve fuel tank was also fitted. 1300 models incorporated a modified rear suspension with a wider track to give increased stability, and this also resulted in a large engine compartment with a restyled lid and vertical number plate mounting. Recessed door handles were also fitted, and the facia control knobs were of plastic. In the same production year the Beetle 1500 was introduced (in October 1966) and was fitted with a 1493cc engine. This model was basically the same as the 1300 but incorporated front wheel disc brakes.

1968 1200 models incorporated fully independent suspension, a collapsible steering column with fitted ignition switch, vertical headlight lenses, a front axle stabiliser, a shorter gear lever and handbrake lever, and an external petrol filler cap. 1300 models incorporated a 12 volt electrical system, two-speed wipers and most of the modifications to 1200 models. In addition a dual braking system was fitted, the bumpers and heater modified, rear lamp clusters enlarged, and a fuel gauge fitted. The luggage and engine compartment lids were also shortened. 1500 models incorporated the modifications of the 1300 plus a modified carburettor and the availability of a semi-automatic transmission.

1969 1200 models incorporated improved front seating, a 12 volt electrical system, hazard warning lights with a facia mounted switch, lockable petrol filler cap, modified ventilation, front bonnet release positioned in the glovebox, and modified control knobs. 1300 models included the 1200 modifications and in addition semi-automatic transmission was available, the rear suspension modified, and radial ply tyres fitted as standard. 1500 models included the 1200 and 1300 modifications and in addition a steering column lock.

1970 1200 models incorporated a modified carburettor, a steering column lock, a dual circuit braking system, and restyled windows. 1300 models included the same modifications but the semi-

automatic transmission was only available to special order. 1500 models continued unchanged and imports ceased in August 1970.

1971 1200 models incorporated a larger windscreen area with a sun roof available as an extra. The windscreen washer reservoir was also enlarged and front and rear towing eyes were fitted. The headlights were wired to the ignition switch. 1300 models included the 1200 modifications, but in addition the engine was modified to increase the power output, front drum brakes were enlarged, and fresh air ventilation was fitted. The 1600 Super Beetle model was introduced in August 1970 (1971 model) and designated the type 1302S. This new model was fitted with a 1584cc engine, and the front luggage compartment lid was 'humped' to provide extra room; the fuel tank was also enlarged. Disc brakes were fitted as standard and the suspension was completely modified. Rear diagonal trailing arms combined with double-jointed axleshaft rear suspension was fitted and the front suspension was changed to MacPherson struts instead of the previous transverse torsion bars.

1972 1200 models were fitted with an enlarged rear window but in all other aspects continued unchanged. 1300 models were also fitted with an enlarged rear window, but in addition the ventilation was modified, a padded steering wheel was fitted, and the wiper/washer switch repositioned to the steering column. The 1584cc 1302S models were fitted with an electronic diagnostic testing socket, but otherwise continued unchanged, and were finally discontinued in August 1972.

1973 1200 models incorporated improved front seating and a repositioned gear lever and handbrake. 1300 models included the 1200 modifications, but in addition the armrests were modified. At the same time the 1300A model was introduced which was a special economy version consisting of the current 1200 model fitted with a 1300 engine. A further two models replaced the discontinued 1302S and were designated the 1303 and 1303S. Both of these models incorporated the 1302S 'humped' body but in addition included a curved windscreen and restyled bonnet. The 1303 was powered by the 1285cc engine and the 1303S by the 1584cc engine. The rear wings were enlarged and incorporated larger rear lamp clusters, and the rear bumper was positioned further back with a shorter exhaust tailpipe. Drum brakes were fitted all round on the 1303 but the 1303S had front disc brakes. Gear ratios were slightly altered and the transmission mountings and gear lever were modified. Seating and ventilation was also modified. Limited production of the GT Beetle with the 1584cc engine also commenced in this production year.

1974 1200 models incorporated box section bumpers and larger rear light clusters. 1300 models included the same modifications as the 1200, as did the 1303 and 1303S but the latter was only available to special order. The 1303 and 1303S models also incorporated modified braking and ventilation.

1975 1200 models incorporated front indicator lamps positioned on the bumper, a modified electrical system, and restyled wheel trims. 1300 models included the 1200 modifications, but in addition the bumpers had towing eyes fitted to them and the bumper mountings were improved. Imports of the 1300 with the basic body ceased in August 1975. 1303 and 1303S models included the 1300 modifications but additionally were fitted with rack and pinion steering. Imports of the 1303 and 1303S saloons ceased in August 1975.

The 1976 1200 model was designated the 1200L and after August 1975 was the only saloon Beetle to be imported into the UK. This model was the 1200 with de luxe trim, heated rear window, fresh air ventilation, reclining seats, reversing lights, a wash-wipe system, and improved seats.

1977 1200L models continued unchanged but the convertible version which was previously discontinued in 1973 was reintroduced and designated the 1303LS Convertible. This model was similar to the 1303S Beetle and incorporated a self-stabilising steering system, wide wheels, front disc brakes, and metallic paintwork.

1978 1200L and 1303LS convertible models continued unchanged and production of both models for the UK ceased in November 1977.

Road Test Data taken from  Autocar

The figures published here are extracts from *Autocar* magazine road tests.

Fuel consumption: The mpg figure is the overall consumption figure for their test period, including performance testing. Many owners will achieve significantly better consumption figures. The formula on the right provides a guide ('**mpg**' refers to the quoted overall test figure).

	1200	1300	1500	1500 semi-automatic	1600
Maximum speed (mph)	72	76	81	74	80
Overall fuel consumption (mpg)	30.9	28.8	27.4	25.1	24.0
Fuel consumption (mpg) at constant:					
30 mph	54	51.3	54.0	42.5	43.5
50 mph	41	38.8	38.5	33.1	34.9
70 mph	28	30.0	29.0	24.7	24.2
Range on full fuel tank (miles)	272	253	241	221	221
Acceleration (seconds):					
0–30 mph	6.2	5.4	5.6	6.2	4.5
0–40 mph	10.2	8.9	8.8	10.6	7.4
0–50 mph	15.8	14.8	14.5	17.1	12.1
0–60 mph	27.5	23.0	21.9	26.8	18.3
0–70 mph	–	54.1	37.0	–	36.6
Standing start ¼ mile	22.9	–	21.9	22.8	20.7
40–60 mph in normal top gear	22.5	23.5	16.5	22.1	19.3

Driving style	Driving conditions		
	severe	average	easy
	−10%	mpg	+10%
	mpg	+10%	+20%
	+10%	+20%	+30%
Hard			
Average			
Gentle			

The data given is for a typical cross-section of the Beetle range only – figures for your particular car may vary.

These figures are copyright of *Autocar*, IPC Transport Press Limited. They are reproduced here with their permission.

In the Driving Seat

Having acquainted ourselves with some of the detailed production modifications of the VW Beetle, it's time to analyse the instruments and controls. Most things are self-explanatory to the experienced motorist, but the following information may be helpful to anyone who has just acquired a Beetle, or for reference purposes.

Instruments and warning lights

The instrument panel layout has remained almost the same throughout the twenty-plus years of importing the Beetle into the UK, with only a few modifications and relocation of some switches.

Ignition warning light and engine cooling warning light

This warning light is located on the speedometer head and is coloured red; on later models it incorporates the letter G for generator. The Beetle engine is air cooled and the cooling fan is fitted to the rear of the dynamo or alternator; therefore if the generator stops, the cooling fan almost stops which results in loss of engine cooling and charging. The warning light serves the dual purpose of informing the driver that the ignition circuit's switched on (even though the engine may not be running) and also indicates whether or not the electrical charging and engine cooling system is functioning correctly.

The light will illuminate when the ignition's initially switched on, but as soon as the engine's started it should fade out. If the engine's allowed to idle slowly, the light may possibly glow especially with a dynamo fitted, but as soon as the engine speed increases it should fade out.

If the light comes on when the engine's turning at above idle speed, first stop the engine and check that the fan belt is still intact. If it is, the generator circuit must be faulty and this should be rectified as soon as possible, though the car may be driven for a limited period provided the battery's in good condition. If the fan belt's loose or broken, tighten or renew it before proceeding.

Oil pressure warning light

This warning light's also located on the speedometer head and is coloured green on early models, red on later models. It informs the driver that normal oil pressure has been reached in the engine when it goes out. When the ignition's initially switched on, the warning light will glow, indicating that there's insufficient oil pressure, but as soon as the engine's started, the light should go out completely.

If the light stays on or comes on when driving, the engine must be stopped immediately; to continue driving is a recipe for an expensive disaster as far as the engine's concerned. The oil level should first be checked by withdrawing the dipstick. Top up the oil if necessary then check that the light goes out when the engine's restarted. If the light still stays on but the engine sounds normal and is not overheated, there's **11**

Typical facia layout on a 1968 model Beetle

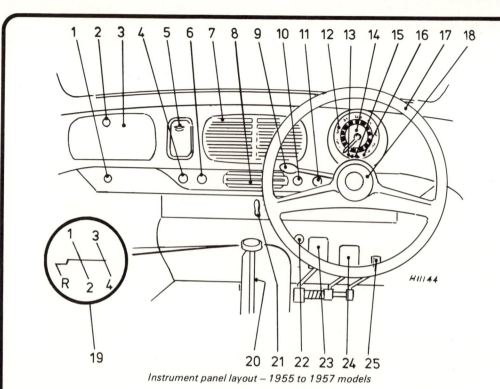

Instrument panel layout – 1955 to 1957 models

1 Luggage compartment release	9 Direction indicator switch	17 Steering wheel
2 Glovebox lock	10 Choke control	18 Horn push
3 Glovebox	11 Ignition/starter switch	19 Gear shift positions
4 Lighting switch	12 Speedometer	20 Gear lever
5 Ashtray	13 Generator and cooling warning light	21 Fuel tap
6 Windscreen wiper switch	14 Headlamp main beam warning light	22 Headlamp dip switch
7 Radio speaker	15 Direction indicator warning light	23 Clutch pedal
8 Radio location	16 Oil pressure warning light	24 Brake pedal
		25 Accelerator pedal

Instrument panel layout – 1964 1200 models

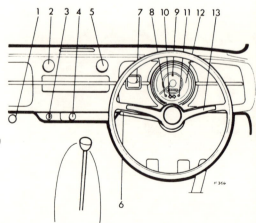

1 Front luggage compartment lock control
2 Light switch
3 Ignition switch
4 Ashtray
5 Windscreen wiper/washer control
6 Direction indicator switch
7 Fuel gauge
8 Generator and cooling system warning light (red)
9 Headlight main beam warning light (blue)
10 Direction indicator warning light (green)
11 Oil pressure warning light (green)
12 Speedometer and mileage recorder/odometer
13 Horn control

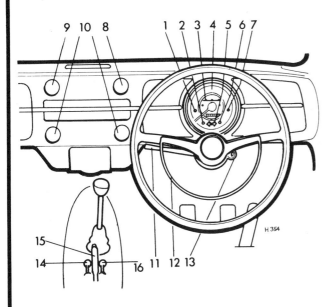

Instrument panel layout – 1968
1300/1500 saloons

1 Converter oil temperature warning
  light (where fitted)
2 Generator and cooling warning light
3 Fuel gauge
4 Speedometer
5 Direction indicator warning light
6 Oil pressure warning light
7 Main beam warning light
8 Windscreen wiper washer
9 Lighting switch
10 Fresh air control knobs
11 Direction indicator switch
12 Horn ring
13 Steering/ignition lock
14 Heat control lever (rear footwell)
15 Parking brake
16 Heat control lever (on/off)

Instrument panel layout – 1970 1300/1500 saloons

1 Sidelamp warning light (where fitted)
2 Heated rear window warning light (where fitted)
3 Generator and cooling warning light
4 Direction indicator warning light
5 Speedometer
6 Fuel gauge
7 Oil pressure warning light
8 Converter oil temperature warning light (where
  fitted)
9 Main beam warning light
10 Tank flap release
11 Luggage compartment release
12 Lighting switch
13 Fresh air control knobs
14 Hazard warning light switch
15 Dual circuit brake warning light (where fitted)
16 Switch for heated rear window (where fitted)
17 Windscreen wiper/washer
18 Direction indicator switch
19 Steering/ignition lock
20 Horn ring
21 Parking brake
22 Heat control lever (rear footwell)
23 Heat control lever (on/off)

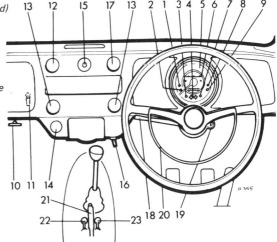

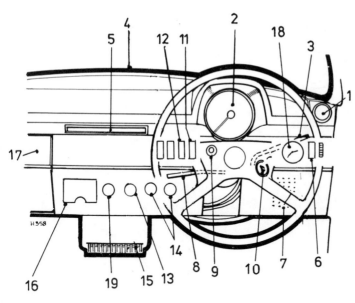

Instrument panel layout –
1973 1303 models

1 Defroster and fresh air
   vents for side windows
2 Speedometer with fuel
   gauge and warning lamps
3 Windscreen wiper and
   washer switch
4 Defroster and fresh air vents
5 Adjustable fresh air vent
6 Lighting switch/instrument
   lights switch
7 Speaker grille
8 Turn signal and dip switch
9 Dual circuit brake warning lamp
10 Steering lock/starter switch
11 Emergency light switch
   with built-in warning lamp
12 Switch for heated rear window
13 Fan switch
14 Fresh air control knobs
15 Fuse box
16 Ashtray
17 Glove compartment
18 Clock
19 Cigar lighter

probably a minor electrical fault, but you should first obtain the advice of the nearest garage. If the engine sounds noisy with abnormal knocking, then to continue running the engine will only add to your problems, and the car should be towed to a garage for investigation.

Main beam warning light

This light's located in the speedometer head and is coloured blue. It illuminates only when the headlights are on main beam, including when the headlight flasher is operated on later models.

Direction indicator warning light

Located on the speedometer head, this warning light's coloured red on early models and green on later models. It flashes on and off when the indicator switch is operated either left or right. If the light flashes quicker than normal at any time, there's probably a faulty bulb in the exterior lamps and this should be rectified as soon as possible.

Handbrake/dual line brake system warning light

On some later models this warning light's located on the facia panel and serves the dual purpose of informing the driver whether the handbrake is applied or not, and whether there's a fault in the braking system. The light should glow when the ignition's switched on and the handbrake's applied, but should go out when the handbrake's released.

If the light glows when driving with the handbrake fully released, stop immediately because a fault is indicated in the dual line braking system and half of the system is probably not functioning. First check that there's sufficient brake fluid in the master cylinder reservoir, then proceed cautiously to the nearest garage to have a complete check of the braking system.

Torque converter oil temperature warning light

Where the semi-automatic transmission is fitted, this light's located on the speedometer head and glows if the torque converter oil temperature exceeds a predetermined limit. This is most likely to occur when driving up a long hill in top gear, and if the light comes on, a lower gear should be selected immediately. If the light still stays on, stop the car on level ground and check the converter oil level and top it up as necessary. On some models the warning lamp displays the letters ATF (Automatic Transmission Fluid).

Fuel gauge

Some later models are fitted with a fuel gauge in the speedometer head, although most models simply had a fuel tap which could be turned to a reserve position when the main fuel supply ceased. The gauge has a reserve section at the bottom of the scale which is approximately equal to 5 litres (1 gallon) of

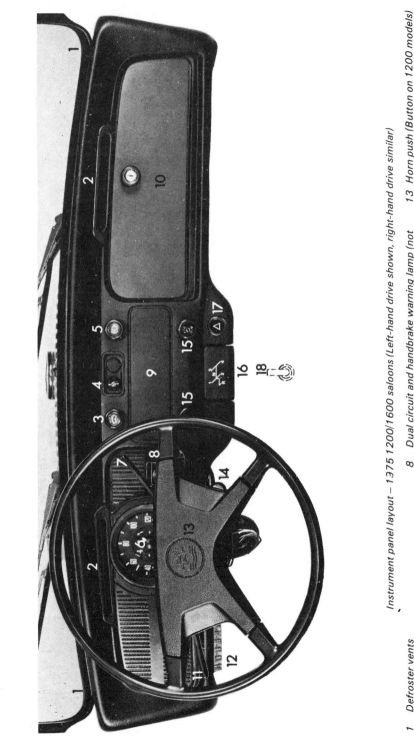

Instrument panel layout — 1375 1200/1600 saloons (Left-hand drive shown, right-hand drive similar)

1 Defroster vents
2 Adjustable vents (1200 L only)
3 Windscreen wiper/washer (1200 only)
4 Fresh air fan (1200 L only)
5 Light switch
6 Speedometer
7 Windscreen wiper/washer lever (1200 L only)

8 Dual circuit and handbrake warning lamp (not all models)
9 Radio aperture
10 Glovebox
11 Direction indicator and headlight beam lever
12 Fusebox and heated rear window switch when fitted

13 Horn push (Button on 1200 models)
14 Ignition switch and steering lock
15 Fresh air controls (1200 L only)
16 Ashtray
17 Hazard warning light switch
18 Fuel tap

15

Fuel tap location

Position 1 – Normal   Position 3 – Off
Position 2 – Reserve

Fuel gauge location in speedometer head (not all models)

Ignition switch location (1971 model shown)

1 – Ignition off   3 – Starting position
2 – Ignition on

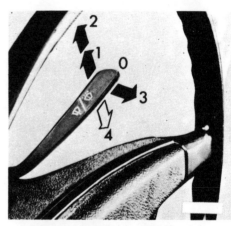

Windscreen wiper/washer switch lever

1 – Slow position   4 – Delay position
2 – Fast position   O – Off position
3 – Wash position

Direction indicator and multi-purpose switch lever

R – Right indicators   A – Headlight beam control
L – Left indicators   O – Off position

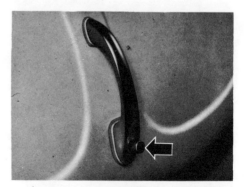

Luggage compartment lid handle location

fuel. The gauge only operates with the ignition switched on.

Switches

Most of the switches on early models are of the push/pull on/off type although later models are fitted with multi-purpose steering column switches.

Ignition switch

On early models this switch is located on the centre section of the facia panel, but on subsequent models is fitted to the steering column and serves as a steering lock as well as an ignition switch. The ignition switch on all models has three positions.

1: With the key in this position the ignition's off and the key may be removed. On models fitted with a steering lock, turn the steering wheel slowly until the internal locking pin engages and locks the steering.

2: With the key in this position the ignition's on and the warning lamps should glow. If the key is difficult to move to this position on models fitted with a steering lock, move the steering wheel slightly to and fro to release the lock. The key should always be in this position when cars fitted with a steering lock are being towed, but disconnect the ignition coil first to prevent it overheating.

3: With the key in this position the starter motor is operated, but once the engine has started the key should be allowed to return to position 2. On some later models the headlights, windscreen wipers, heater fan, and heated rear window (where fitted) are automatically switched off when the key is turned to position 3 in order to provide maximum battery current for the starter motor. On all but very early models the ignition switch incorporates a non-repeat function whereby if the engine does not start after returning the key to position 2, the key must first be returned to position 1 before attempting to start the engine again. This prevents accidental operation of the starter with the engine running.

Windscreen wiper switch

This switch is mounted on the facia panel on most models but is substituted by a steering column stalk switch on some later models. The original switch is a push/pull type but later types incorporate a washer system. On this type the switch is rotated to switch on the wipers and the centre button pressed to operate the washer.

Where a steering column switch is fitted, the operation is as shown in the accompanying illustration.

1: Wipers operate slowly or, on some models, until the lever is released.

2: Wipers operate fast.

3: By pulling the lever towards the steering **17**

Semi-automatic transmission selector lever positions

A – 1975 models   *B – 1971 models*

wheel, water is sprayed onto the windscreen, and on some models the wipers operate two or three times.

4: This function is not included on all models, but where fitted the wipers operate every 10 seconds.

Direction indicator and multi-purpose switch

The stalk lever switch is located on the left-hand side of the steering column, and on early models simply operated the indicators. On later models it incorporated additional functions as shown in the accompanying illustration. Normal movement up or down operates the right or left indicator lamps in the identical manner to the previous switch, and the lever automatically cancels when the car assumes a straight direction again. If temporary indication is required the lever should be moved until slight resistance is felt; on releasing the lever from this position it will return immediately to the cancel position.

To operate the headlamp full beam using the switch, pull the lever towards the steering wheel; with the lever pushed away from the steering wheel the headlight dipped beam will be in operation provided the facia switch is on.

Luggage compartment lid release

On early models this is located just beneath the facia panel and on convertible models a lock is provided. Later models had the lever located inside the lockable glovebox.

After releasing the lock, depress the push button on the front of the lid to open it. Always make sure that the lid catch is fully engaged before driving again.

Automatic transmission selector

On models fitted with semi-automatic transmission the following instructions must be adhered to.

Unlike the normal manual Beetle gearbox the semi-automatic transmission incorporates a 3-speed fully synchronized gearbox. The selector lever positions are shown in the accompanying illustration; the three forward speeds are L (low), 1, and 2 and the reverse gear R. The lever is retained in the N (Neutral) position by spring pressure which must be pressed against in order to move the lever to the L and R positions. Additionally the lever must be depressed in order to reach the R position on early versions without a P (Park) position. Where a P position is fitted the lever must be depressed in order to reach it.

N (Neutral)

The engine can only be started when the lever's in this position. No power is transmitted to the driving wheels and if you're being towed or pushed you should always locate the lever in this position.

L (Low)

This position covers speeds from 0 to 55 km/hr (0 to 35 mph) and should generally be used when towing or traversing difficult or hilly terrain.

1

This position covers speeds from 0 to 90 km/hr (0 to 55 mph) and should normally be used for moving off, medium gradients, and when maximum acceleration is required for overtaking etc.

2

This position covers normal driving speeds and can be selected soon after moving off; it is in order to keep the transmission in this gear even in slow moving town traffic.

R (Reverse)

This must only be selected with the car stationary and the engine idling.

P (Park)

Where fitted this position must also be selected only when the car's stationary because the rear wheels are mechanically locked. When engaging the lock always apply the handbrake first.

When starting the engine from cold it is advisable to let the engine run at a fast idle for about a minute before selecting a gear; this will allow the torque converter fluid to circulate and will enable a smooth selection to be made. Always apply the footbrake before selecting a gear as there will be a certain amount of 'creep' when the gear is engaged.

Engine idling

As a safety precaution always apply the handbrake and select neutral (N) if the engine is to be left idling for an extended period, such as when checking the ignition timing or carburettor adjustments.

Towing

The car can be towed without any restrictions with the selector lever in N (Neutral). If the battery's flat the engine may be started by towing the car with the selector lever in position L at about 25 km/hr (16 mph). It's not possible to push start the car at speeds lower than this.

Filling Station Facts

Forgetting about the actual servicing and mechanical maintenance of your car for the time being, there are some things which are so simple they're likely to get overlooked; but they're not only an important part of the maintenance of your car – they're vital for its safety and reliability too. Two of these items – oil and tyres – you can check if necessary whenever you visit a petrol station. We've set out here the absolute minimum of information you need to know.

Topping up oil

Whenever you top up the oil level, always try to use the same grade and brand, and do avoid using cheap oil – the initial saving will probably be lost in increased engine wear over a prolonged period – or perhaps a short one!

When checking the oil level, ensure that the car's standing on level ground. Take out the dipstick from the right-hand side of the engine, wipe it clean, then replace it fully. Pull it out again and note the oil level. Under no circumstances should the level be allowed to drop below the minimum mark. If additional oil is required, unscrew the oil filler cap and pour in more oil until the level is at the full mark on the dipstick, but avoid over-filling the engine, and wipe away any spilt oil. The use of a plastic funnel is an advantage when pouring oil into the filler pipe. Screw the cap on firmly and refit the dipstick when completed.

Tyre pressures

When checking tyre pressures don't forget to check the pressure in the spare – in the event of a puncture you could be in for a 'let down'! If you're affluent enough to have your own tyre pressure gauge, always use this to check the pressures – garage gauges aren't always terribly accurate and it's essential that the pressures are right to ensure the correct handling of the car when steering and braking.

The pressure in the spare wheel should be more than that in the wheels in use where it operates the windscreen washer, but it must never exceed 42 psi, and when the spare is used the pressure should be

Engine oil dipstick location (1971 model shown)

Petrol filler cap location (later models)

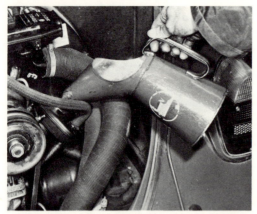

Topping up the engine oil level

Minimum and maximum marks on the engine oil level dipstick

Checking the tyre pressures with a hand gauge

adjusted at the earliest opportunity.

Remember that tyre pressures can only be checked accurately when the tyres are cold. Any tyre that's travelled more than a mile or so will show a pressure increase of several pounds per square inch (psi) — maybe more than 5 psi after a longer run. So a certain amount of 'guesstimation' comes into checking tyres if they're warm.

Since the pressure won't increase for any reason other than heat, the least you can do is to ensure that the pressures in the two front tyres are equal. (The same applies to the two back tyres, but remember that their pressure should be different from the front).

If one tyre of a pair has a low pressure when hot, bring it up to the pressure of the other at the same end of the car; if they're both below the recommended cold pressure although warm, the safest thing to do is to bring them up to about 3 psi above it, to allow for cooling.

Self-service garages

Many garages now operate on a self-service basis so that the customer's subjected to the intricacies of refuelling his or her own vehicle. Regulars to this type of establishment need no introduction to its methods of operation and can usually be seen going through the routine at high speed like well-oiled robots. To the newcomer, the operation of the various kinds of pump can at first be confusing, but don't panic! Carefully read each instruction on the pump in turn before attempting to work it. When refuelling, insert the nozzle fully into the car's filler tube and try to regulate the fuel flow at an even rate so that it's not too fast. Most pumps now have an automatic flow-back valve mechanism fitted in them, which prevents any surplus petrol making a speedy exit from the filler neck all over the unsuspecting operator. On completion, don't forget to refit your petrol filler cap!

QUICK-CHECK CHART

FUEL OCTANE RATING
1200 engines
1300, 1500, and 1600 engines

87 octane (2 star) min
91 octane (3 star) min

FUEL TANK CAPACITY
1302S models
All other models

42 litres (9·2 gallons)
40 litres (8·8 gallons)

ENGINE OIL TYPE
All models

SAE 20W/40 or 20W/50 multigrade

QUANTITY OF OIL REQUIRED TO BRING LEVEL FROM MINIMUM TO MAXIMUM ON DIPSTICK
All models

1·25 litres (2·2 pints)

TYRE PRESSURES

Recommended pressures in psi (kgf/cm^2)–cold tyres

Tyre size	1 or 2 occupants		3 to 5 occupants	
	Front	Rear	Front	Rear
560–15 4PR and 600–15L 4PR (Crossply)	16 (1·1)	27 (1·9)	18 (1·3)	27 (1·9)
155 SR 15 (Radial)	18 (1·3)	27 (1·9)	18 (1·3)	27 (1·9)

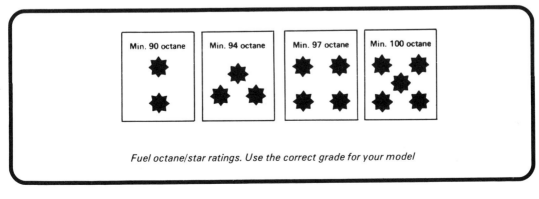

Fuel octane/star ratings. Use the correct grade for your model

In an Emergency

If you're fairly new to motoring, the chances are you've never experienced the misfortune of a puncture, or a malfunction with the engine, causing a premature (but hopefully temporary) halt to your journey.

In the early days of motoring, 'roadside rebuilds' weren't too uncommon a sight, but fortunately over the years the car has developed into a comparatively sophisticated and reliable means of transport. However, today's motorist still has the occasional mishap and, even if it's only a puncture, it pays to be prepared.

Always carry the wheel brace and jack supplied with the car under the rear seat and in the luggage compartment, and of course make sure that the spare tyre's kept properly inflated at all times to at least the highest specified pressure. The correct use of the jack is described later on.

Minor malfunctions of the engine can often be repaired at the roadside, but one or two basic tools may be required, and these can easily be stored away in the front luggage compartment until needed. It's obviously not possible to carry a complete set of spare parts around with you, but again one or two of the more easily used items can be stored in the luggage compartment. The sort of things you should carry are:

Spark plug, clean and with the correct gap
HT lead and plug cap — long enough to reach the plug furthest from the dietributor
Set of the main light bulbs
Pocket tyre pressure gauge
Spare fuses
Distributor rotor, condenser and contact points
Fan belt
Roll of insulating tape
Extension light and lead with crocodile clips
Clean lint-free cloth
Breakdown triangle
Tow rope
First aid box
Spare set of keys (but not kept in the car)
De-icer aerosol (during winter)
This Handbook or Haynes Workshop Manual
List of VW agents

If and when a breakdown occurs it's not always in a convenient spot. If the road's narrow or busy, poorly lit, or you're on a bend, then a minor problem may develop into a major catastrophe unless you take action to warn the oncoming and following traffic. If you can't pull off the road, first switch on the hazard warning lights (where fitted) and if you're on a blind bend, place a warning triangle a suitable distance, say 100 feet (30 metres), behind your vehicle to warn following traffic.

We'll mention here just four other items for emergency use which it might make you feel happier to have on board. The first is a 'universal' temporary

A box like this is useful for keeping your emergency repairs kit together

If you want to carry emergency petrol, use an approved safety can of the type shown here. The detachable spout makes pouring easy, too

An 'Instant Spare' aerosol in use on a flat tyre

fan belt which can be fitted without loosening any bolts, and which will enable you to get going again quickly in the event of a belt breakage, and to fit a proper replacement belt at your leisure.

The second 'get-you-home' device is an 'instant' puncture repair in the form of an aerosol can. The nozzle is screwed on to the tyre valve, and releases sealant to seal the leak, together with gas to reinflate the tyre. It's suitable for tubed or tubeless tyres, and will at the very least allow you to drive to a garage without getting your hands dirty.

Our third additional suggestion is a temporary windscreen. If you've ever suffered a shattered screen, you'll know what a nightmare it can be trying to drive the car, especially in bad weather. If you haven't, take our word for it! One of the roll-up type of polyester temporary screens is quick and easy to fit, leaves driving unaffected, and wipers and washers can be used normally. When not in use its thin container stows neatly in a corner of the luggage compartment or on the back shelf.

It's not normally necessary to carry extra fuel with you in this country, but if you do feel you need a spare gallon or so in the luggage compartment for emergencies, we strongly recommend the use of one of the special cans made for the purpose. These are

not only designed to be safe in the event of an accident, and leakproof, but they also generally have a screw-on spout which makes it much easier to get the petrol into the car's filler neck if you have to!

Changing a wheel

Should a puncture occur, try to park off the road to change the wheel, choosing a firm level spot. Check that the handbrake's fully engaged and select reverse or 1st gear if both rear wheels are remaining on the ground. On automatic transmission models select P (Park) where possible. As an added precaution, check all wheels not being changed.

Remove the jack from beneath the rear seat by lifting the rear seat cushion; there's no need to remove the cushion completely. Open the luggage compartment lid and remove the spare wheel and tools. On models fitted with a windscreen washer bottle the pressure hose must be unscrewed from the spare wheel. On later models the bottle is clamped to the wheel, and in this case, place the wheel on the front apron while the two retaining wedges are removed. On models fitted with headlight washers, disconnect the pump wires, pull the filler cap off, and place the bottle on the bumper before removing the wheel.

An emergency windscreen is fitted in seconds and can save untold discomfort

Carefully prise the wheel cap from the wheel to be changed using the puller or tapered bar supplied with the tool kit, then loosen (but don't remove) the wheel nuts or bolts using the wheel brace supplied. Where sports wheels are fitted, remove the centre plate and the plastic caps from the bolt heads before loosening them.

The jacking point on the corner of the car to be raised will probably be partially blocked with dirt, so clean this out before inserting the jack arm. Insert the jack arm into the square hole making sure that it's fully entered then operate the jack until the wheel is clear of the ground. Two basic types of jack are provided and the operation of these is shown in the accompanying illustrations.

Unscrew the wheel nuts, remove the wheel and fit the spare in its place. Tighten the wheel nuts progressively and evenly, but there's no need to fully tighten them until the car's standing on all four wheels. Lower the jack and remove it, then using the wheel brace tighten the nuts or bolts in diagonal sequence; the brace is designed to provide the correct torque if used by a normal healthy adult, but for peace of mind they can be checked with a torque wrench. The correct setting is as follows:

1302S models	*108 lbf ft (15 kgf m)*
All other models	*94 lbf ft (13 kgf m)*

The pressure in the new spare must be checked at the very first opportunity after repair to ensure that it's up to the specified figure at least.

Towing

If you ever have to tow another vehicle and your Beetle isn't fitted with a towing hitch, the only safe place to connect the tow rope is to the bumper, but this is not recommended if the car being towed is anything larger than the average small car.

When towing, try to keep the tow rope taut between the vehicles; it's always helpful to the following traffic if an 'On Tow' notice is displayed at the rear of the towed vehicle. Keep to the nearside of the road as much as possible.

Should you have the misfortune to end up on the tail end of a tow rope at any time and you own an early Beetle without a tow hitch, the bumper is again the best place to fix the tow rope, though it can be attached to the front axle tube. Some models are provided with a towing eye on the lower axle tube and on later models the eye is attached to the front bumper.

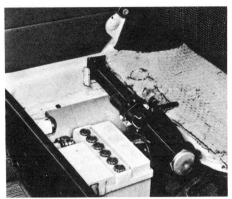

Jack location beneath the rear seat

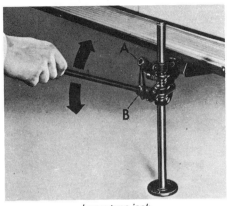

Lever type jack

A – position to raise car   B – position to lower car

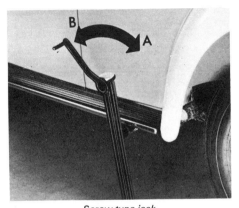

Screw type jack

A – direction to raise car   B – direction to lower car

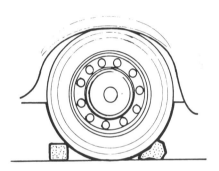

Always chock the wheel before jacking

Towing eye location on some models

A – Front,   *B – Rear*

Before being towed check that the tow rope's securely fastened, and isn't interfering with the steering or suspension when under load. Always make sure that the steering lock where fitted is disengaged, and if it's not possible to switch on the ignition remember to use hand signals. Fix the 'On Tow' notice to the rear of your car to warn the following traffic, but don't block your line of vision. Try to keep the towing rope reasonably taut by slightly applying the brakes when necessary, especially when going down hill or stopping.

If your car's fitted with the semi-automatic transmission, move the selector lever to the N (Neutral) position and retain it there during the towing operation.

Fuses and light bulbs

A blown fuse or a failed light bulb can cause real problems if it occurs during a journey (in the case of an exterior light it's also illegal). We've therefore classed these as 'emergencies' and we'll deal with their rectification here.

Fuses

Some of the electrical circuits are protected against overloading by being directed through a fuse. The main fusebox is mounted beneath the facia panel on all models though the number of fuses has varied.

On early models with a six volt electrical system four fuses are located under the dashboard and the circuits protected comprise the following:-

Fuse 1   Number plate light, O/S rear light
Fuse 2   N/S rear light, Front sidelights
Fuse 3   Direction indicators, Stop lights
Fuse 4   Windscreen wipers, Horn

In addition in-line fuses located near the fuel tank protected the headlight main beams.

Later models with the six volt system have eight fuses located under the dashboard and near the fuel tank in two blocks of four. The circuits protected are as follows:

Block 1 (near fuel tank)
1   Main beam (right)
2   Main beam (left) and warning light
3   Low beam (right)
4   Low beam (left)
Block 2 (dashboard)
1   Interior light and horn
2   Screen wiper, stop lights and indicators
3   Sidelights and tail light (right)
4   Tail light (left) and number plate light

Subsequently the two blocks of fuses were changed for a single eight fuse block under the

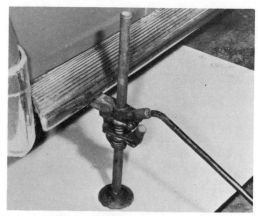
Early type jack in position

Fusebox location on 12 volt, 10 fuse system

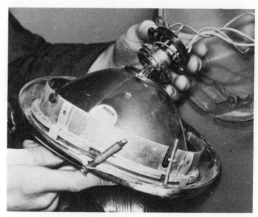
Removing a headlamp bulb

Additional in-line fuse location on some models (1970 model shown)

A – Reversing lamps
B – Selector automatic transmission shift switch

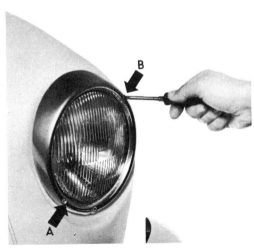

Headlight adjustment screw locations – not to be altered when removing headlight bulbs

A – Horizontal adjustment   B – Vertical adjustment

instrument panel; the circuits protected were as follows:

1 Windscreen wiper, indicators, horn, stop lights
2 Main beams (left) and warning light
3 Main beam (right)
4 Low beam (left)
5 Low beam (right)
6 Sidelight (left)
7 Sidelight and number plate lamp (right)
8 Interior light and radio

The first 12 volt system included ten fuses in one block beneath the facia panel and the circuits protected are as follows:

1 Horn, indicators, stop lights, fuel gauge, dual circuit warning light, automatic transmission shift, heated rear window
2 Screen wipers, stop lights
3 Main beam (left) and warning light
4 Main beam (right)
5 Dipped beam (left)
6 Dipped beam (right)
7 Sidelights front and rear (right or left), number plate light
8 Sidelights front and rear (right or left), number plate light
9 Radio, interior light, headlamp flasher, hazard warning light
10 Interior light, headlamp flasher, radio

The 12 volt system with twelve fuses in one block covers different circuits according to the model; however the following is a typical layout:

1 Front sidelights and right tail light
2 Left tail light
3 Main beam (left), main beam warning light
4 Main beam (right)
5 Low beam (left)
6 Low beam (right)
7 Spare
8 Hazard flasher system
9 Headlight flasher, interior light
10 Stop lights, horn
11 Screen wiper
12 Gauges and warning lights

Additionally on some models there are separate fuses as follows:

Reversing light fuse on the fan housing in the engine compartment
Heated rear window fuse beneath the rear seat
Automatic transmission shift fuse in the engine compartment adjacent to the reversing light fuse

Always renew a fuse with one of equivalent value and, if the new one blows within a short space of **27**

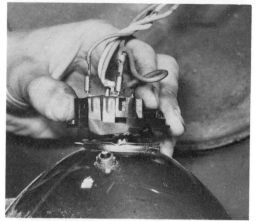

Sidelight bulb location and contact strip

Removing a direction indicator bulb

Removing a rear light cluster lens

Removing the number plate lens and bulb holder

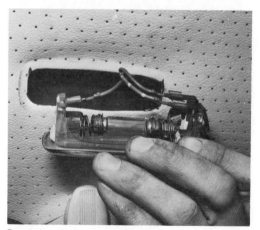

Removing the interior light bulb

Showing access to the speedometer head instrument bulbs, also location of in-line fuses

time, have the circuit checked out by your VW agent. Never replace a fuse with an object such as a nail or a piece of metal foil – it could lead to serious trouble and even a fire.

Headlight bulb renewal

Unscrew the bottom rim retaining screw, pull the lower part away, then unhook it from the top. Do not disturb the beam adjustment screws shown in the illustration. On early headlights fitted with bulbs, the reflector assembly will come away with the rim, but on later ones and sealed beam units, the rim alone will come away. On early models pull the bulb holder from the reflector and disconnect the wiring connector. On later models, unscrew the retaining screws if fitted and remove the unit, then pull off the three-pin connector, twist the retaining ring and remove the bulb. On the halogen type bulb the clips must be unhooked before removing the bulb. To remove the sealed beam unit unscrew the three inner rim retaining screws and lift the unit out; the three-pin connector can then be disconnected.

When refitting a headlight bulb, make sure that the engagement lugs are entered correctly, and especially with halogen type bulbs, try not to touch the glass as this can shorten the bulbs' life. If it's handled, wipe the glass using a soft clean rag moistened with methylated spirit.

Sidelight (parking light) bulb renewal (non-sealed beam)

This bulb's located in the rear of the headlight reflector and therefore the reflector must be removed first. Pull off the main connector then remove the bulb and bulb holder where fitted. Refit the bulb in the reverse manner but make sure that the contact strip on the connector is firmly against the bulb.

Direction indicator bulb renewal (and parking light-sealed beam)

On the semaphore type indicators operate the arm and then unscrew the strip cover retaining screw; the cover can then be lifted sufficient to remove the festoon type bulb.

On the flasher type indicators and sealed beam type parking lights, remove the cover screw and lift the cover off. Depress and twist the bulb to remove it.

Refit in the reverse manner and make sure that the cover locates correctly on the sealing gasket.

Rear combination light bulbs renewal

Unscrew the lens retaining screws and remove the lens, then depress and twist the bulb to remove it. The upper bulb is for direction indication, the centre bulb for stop lights and tail lights, and the bottom bulb, when fitted, is for the reversing lights.

The stop and tail light bulb can only be refitted in one position, ie with the locating pin nearest the glass downwards.

Rear number plate light bulb renewal

Open the engine lid, remove the two retaining screws, and withdraw the lens and bulb holder. Prise the bulb holder from the lens and depress and twist the bulb to remove it. When refitting the bulb make sure that the grommet locates correctly.

Headlamp fitted with a Halogen bulb

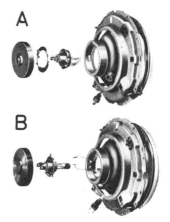

Later type bulb arrangements

A – Normal bulb   B – Halogen bulb

Sealed beam unit arrangement

A – Outer rim retaining screw
B – Inner rim retaining screw locations
C – Headlight beam adjustment screw location

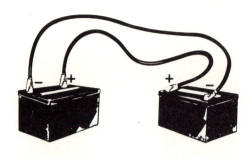

Jumper cable connections

Negative (-) to (-) negative (Black)
Positive (+) to (+) positive (Red)

Interior light bulb renewal

Carefully prise the lens away from the roof, taking care not to mark the headlining, then extract the festoon type bulb from between the spring clips. Refit the bulb in the reverse manner and press the lens firmly into the roof panel.

Instrument illumination and warning lamp bulb renewal

Open the luggage compartment lid and remove the bulkhead backing panel; the bulbs can then be removed from the rear of the speedometer head.

Emergency starting

If for any reason your battery's flat and it doesn't have sufficient power to turn the engine, then the use of jumper leads is probably your best bet provided you have access to another battery or you can persuade a passing motorist to oblige. Remember that you shouldn't connect a 12 volt battery to a 6 volt system unless the battery has exterior inter-cell connectors making it possible to tap off the 6 volts.

Although the jumper leads are ideal for transferring power from one battery to another over a short period, it's of utmost importance that they're connected properly or damage may result. The positive (+) terminals of each battery must be interconnected using the same cable whilst the negative (-) terminals are similarly connected using the other cable as shown in the accompanying illustration. **Don't** interchange these connections!

Connect the leads to the slave battery first then to the battery of the car to be started. This reduces the chance of sparks in the vicinity of the charged battery which may be giving off explosive hydrogen gas!

Save It!

For the owner-driver motoring never has been and probably never will be a cheap pastime. If a car isn't used much, then the running costs will be low, but the few miles travelled in it are comparatively expensive when the initial cost plus subsequent depreciation are taken into account. But obviously the more you use your car, then the maintenance and running costs must correspondingly increase. So you can't win – or can you? Since money is fairly close to most people's hearts, any chances of reducing the annual motoring bill are not to be sniffed at – but how **can** we reduce the costs? Let's talk about some of the most important items to be considered from the economic point of view.

Maintenance

To start with, the car must be kept in a good state of tune in order to give the maximum performance combined with reliability. Although a car may start without too much bother each day and transport you from A to B without giving trouble, it may well be operating quite ineffeciently and therefore indirectly adding to your costs.

The various components on a car that need regular servicing will continue to function without complaint when neglected but the working life of these components is invariably shortened so they'll need renewal before it should be necessary.

If you normally take your car to a garage for servicing then you'll no doubt have noticed the ever increasing costs of the labour charges. Unless you can be sure that the garage people you deal with are honourable types, how do you know if the work listed as completed has been carried out properly, if at all?

One of the aims of this book is to encourage owners to do their own servicing which, though you may never have handled even a spanner, is well within the capabilities of the average person. The ironmongery lying beneath your car's bodywork is not nearly so technical and formidable as it may appear.

With a small initial outlay in costs for some basic tools you could, over a period of time, save yourself a considerable sum of money and be a more complete motorist, simply by doing your own basic service tasks. You'll also be able to shop around for the parts required and probably obtain them at cheaper prices than those charged by your garage.

Driving habits

Bad driving habits can very often contribute towards inefficient motoring and add to its costs. Usually a driver develops a habit over a period of time and is quite unaware of the fault. Things like erratic use of the throttle, leaving the handbrake slightly on, waiting too long before changing up or down a gear, forgetting to push the choke knob in, cornering too fast, and excessive use of the brakes all add to the cost of motoring.

Tyres

Without any doubt whatever, a radial tyre will give you much better value for money than a crossply because, although it will cost a bit more to buy, it will last a great deal longer. Remould tyres can give good service, but they have their limitations when used for family motoring; remould radials now have a more reliable reputation than they had when they first appeared on the market, but sometimes give a bit of trouble when trying to balance them.

So, what have we learnt so far? Only that in the broadest terms the more you pay for your tyres, the better value for money you'll get. If you want the best in roadholding and tyre life, buy radials; if you want reasonable tyre life, but aren't quite so worried about the roadholding under adverse conditions, buy crossply; if you want a good runabout tyre, and aren't thinking of high speeds or long journeys, buy radial remoulds but remember they may give a bit of steering wheel 'shimmy' if used on the front; if you want the cheapest tyre which still complies with the **31**

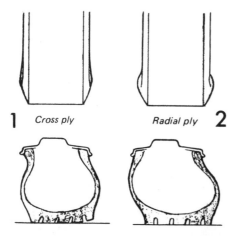

1   *Cross ply*   *Radial ply*   2

*A cross-section of a cross-ply tyre (left) and a radial
ply tyre (right)
The difference in the construction of the two types of
tyre gives them very different characteristics. The
cross-ply (1) has a uniformly strong tread and wall
bracing. This gives it better cushioning properties but
allows some deformation on bad surfaces and
cambers. The radial ply type (2) has a supple wall and
a firmly braced tread, ensuring that the maximum area
of tread is kept in contact with the road despite
suspension angle changes and road camber effects.*

law in safety standards, buy remould crossplies.

Regraded tyres are sometimes available (they
used to be known as remould quality or RQ), these
are tyres which may have the very slightest defects in
the tread pattern or moulding, but are otherwise
perfect. If you get the chance to buy these, buy them
– to all intents and purposes they're as good as a new
tyre.

It's not generally realized that the major tyre
manufacturers also produce tyres under a less well
known name at a somewhat cheaper price. These are
first class buys too – ask any tyre dealer.

Talking of tyre dealers, it's worth mentioning that
they're the people to go to if you're intent on saving
money (and who isn't these days?). Unless there's a
'special offer' going, the most expensive place to get
your tyres will normally be your local garage.

Now first let's just briefly consider how to make
tyres last. Firstly, keep them inflated properly (see
Filling Station Facts for the correct pressures).
Second, drive sensibly (ie no race-track starts or
cornering). Third, make sure the wheels are balanced
properly (a job for a garage or tyre specialist).

Batteries

Next to tyres, batteries are the most commonly

found parts sold by specialists. A top quality battery
may cost up to three times the price of the cheapest
one that'll fit your car.

Once again, price is related to the quality of the
product, but isn't necessarily directly proportional. A
battery with a twelve month guarantee ought to last
that long and a little bit more, but batteries always
seem to fail at embarrassing or inconvenient times so
it's worthwhile getting something a little bit better.
Many of the accessory shops and tyre dealers sell
good quality batteries with two or three year
guarantees. Buy one of these – it'll be worthwhile in
the long run and still cost quite a bit less than the
dearest ones around. And if you look after it, it'll look
after you, too.

Exhaust systems

The average car gets through several exhaust
systems in the course of its life, the actual number
depending on the sort of journeys for which the car's
used (lots of short journeys will mean condensation
remaining inside the exhaust system and helping it to
rust out more quickly).

The best place to go when your Beetle needs a
replacement exhaust (or maybe just part of the
system) is one of the specialist 'exhaust centres'
which have sprung up in recent years. They keep huge
stocks to fit most mass-produced cars, and offer free
fitting as well as discount prices on the parts
themselves. You'll almost certainly show a
worthwhile saving compared with getting your VW
dealer to fit the exhaust (which will involve labour
charges as well).

If you're planning to keep your car for several
years it would certainly be worth thinking about an
exhaust system made from stainless steel. It'll
normally cost you considerably more than an ordinary
mild steel replacement, but on the other hand should
last the remainder of the car's life. If you're interested,
talk it over with one of the exhaust specialists –
they're usually stockists of the stainless steel kind too.

Lubricants and the like

Good cheap engine oils are available, but
because it's so difficult to find out which cheap ones
are good, it's safest to stay clear of them. There are
plenty of good multigrade engine oils on the market
and quite a few are available at sensible prices from
the DIY motoring and accessory shops.

Unless circumstances should force you to, don't
buy oil in pint or half-litre cans. This is the most
expensive way of buying, particularly if it's from a
filling station. The big 5-litre (they used to be one
gallon) cans are adequate for most purposes, and
contain just about the right amount for an engine oil
change. If your pride and joy happens to be a bit of an

oil burner, you may need an extra can for topping up between oil changes.

Oil is also available in larger drums (which can be fitted with a tap) sometimes at an even bigger price saving. A telephone call or visit to nearby wholesalers may well prove worthwhile.

Antifreeze is always cheaper if you go to the motoring shops, but bulk buying doesn't normally apply because you never need to buy it in any real quantity.

As for greases, brake fluid, etc, you'll save a little at the motoring shops but again you'll never need large quantities – just make sure you buy something that's good quality.

Fuel

Your car's designed to run on a particular grade of fuel (star rating). Don't buy fuel that's of a higher rating than this, because you're wasting your money. On the other hand, if you buy a lower rating fuel your engine performance (and probably your engine too) will suffer. If you *are* forced to buy inferior fuel, drive carefully until you can get the correct grade; in these circumstances it's also beneficial to retard the ignition by a couple of degrees, but you've got the bother of resetting it again later.

Additives

Oil and fuel additives have been with us for a long time and no doubt will be around for many years to come. It's pretty unlikely that there are any bad additives around, but there's not a great deal of evidence to suggest that there are many good ones.

The major oil manufacturers will tell you that their oils are adequate on their own, in which case you'll only need additives if the oil you're using isn't much good. A fuel additive of the upper cylinder lubricant type is generally accepted as a good thing, one of its main functions being to prevent carbon building up around the piston rings and ring grooves, which means that the piston rings can seal more effectively.

Economy devices

If we could believe everything published about economy devices, we'd be able to fit the lot and end up with a car that would save more fuel than it used! Obviously this isn't going to happen, and the evidence produced by the motoring magazines doesn't lend much weight to the various manufacturers' arguments. If you're considering fitting any of these items (which range from manifold modifiers to spark boosters and fuel pressure regulators) try to get hold of some independent reports before parting with your money.

Vacuum gauge

Also known as a performance gauge or fuel consumption gauge, this can loosely be termed an economy device because its purpose is to tell you how to use performance in the most efficient way. An engine that's running efficiently will be using all the fuel/air mixture in the inlet manifold for any given throttle opening, and in doing so it causes a fairly high suction past the throttle butterfly. The maximum suction it can produce varies, but could be over 20 inches of mercury (that's around 10 psi) relative to atmospheric pressure. If you've got one of these gauges, (and there's some information about fitting one in *The Personal Touch*) try to drive with the maximum vacuum reading all the time and you'll certainly save some money on fuel.

Engine tuning

This term is much misused; it simply means getting the best performance and economy (or sometimes one at the expense of the other) from the standard engine. You'll have a job to improve on the specifications and settings laid down by the car manufacturers, so these must be your obvious guidelines. Different size jets are available for the carburettor if you're after a little more economy or performance.

Regular maintenance is the most important factor in keeping the engine in a good state of tune (eg spark plugs, distributor points, ignition timing, carburettor adjustments, air cleaners, valve clearances), but take care that things like over-adjusted brakes don't mar this. If you can look after all these things, the rest's up to you as the driver.

Smiths Industries 'Milemiser' monitors fuel consumption through intake manifold vacuum

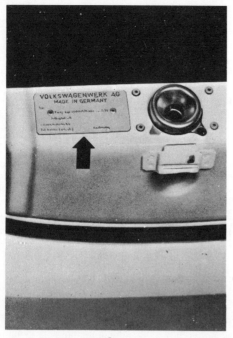

A

B

C

Vehicle identification locations

A – Luggage compartment
B – Rear frame
C – Engine crankcase

Roof racks

The ever-faithful roof rack has proved a boon to so many motorists for the extra holiday luggage, but how often do you see cars being driven around with an empty roof rack still attached? Many estimates have been made of the increase in fuel consumption caused by a roof rack due to wind resistance and the accepted figure is around 10%; with a loaded rack, this figure can be as high as 30%. The moral, then, is obvious – don't use a roof rack unless you have to, and always remove it when it's not in use.

Insurance

Like some of the other things we've discussed, the service you're going to get from your insurance company will be related to the cost of the cover obtained. A cheap policy's good until you need to make a claim, and then the sort of snags you're going to come across are 'How do I get hold of an assessor to inspect the damage?' or 'How will it affect my No Claims Bonus?'

There are one or two legitimate ways of reducing the policy premium, perhaps by insuring for 'owner driver only', or 'two named drivers', or an agreement to pay the first £20 or so of any claim. Many large companies have a discount scheme for their employees if they use the same insurance company; this also applies to bank and Civil Service employees. You may also get a better bargain by insuring through one of the Motoring Associations if you're a member.

What it all adds up to is: (1) Insure well: (2) See what you can get in the way of discounts; and (3) Find out exactly what you're covered for.

The car itself

It's almost a forgone conclusion that the smaller-engined models will be more economical than those with the larger engines, until you look at comparative fuel consumption figures. Maybe your model has a smaller engine, but when the car's well loaded you're going to have to use the gearbox more. This means higher engine revs, more wear and tear and consequently less economy, so never rule out a larger-engined model because you think it's bound to use more fuel. Where you *might* save a little is on replacement parts (where these are related to engine size), and insurance.

Buying spare parts

Apart from the oils and greases which you're going to need, it won't be long before you have to buy a few bits and pieces to keep things running smoothly. Please do remember to clean up any parts which are traded-in on exchange basis (eg brake shoes) and, wherever possible, check that any replacement parts look the same as the old ones, either by direct comparison if this can be done, or by reference to any of the illustrations in the appropriate Section of this book.

Spare parts and accessories are available from many sources, but the following should act as a good guide when they're required.

Officially appointed garages: Although dealers should be able to supply just about everything for your car, it will generally be found that the prices are higher than you *need* pay.

Accessory shops: These are usually the best places for you to get distributor contact breaker points, oil filters, brake shoes, spark plugs, fan belts, lubricants, touch-up paints etc – the very things you're going to need for the general servicing of your car. They also sell general accessories and charge lower prices, but, what's equally important, they have convenient opening hours and can often be found not too far from home.

Motor factors: Good factors will stock all the more important components of the engine, gearbox, suspension, and braking systems, and often provide guaranteed parts on an exchange basis. They're particularly useful to the more advanced do-it-yourself motorist.

Vehicle identification numbers

When obtaining spare parts (and sometimes accessories), the very least you must know is the model and year of manufacture of your car. For some items this is all you need to know, but there will soon come a time when you're asked for the engine number or chassis number (which you'd always meant to make a note of but just didn't get around to!). Make a note of these numbers now, in your diary or in the back of this book.

The main identification plate is in the front luggage compartment near the lock and the information includes the model types and chassis number.

The chassis number is also stamped on the rear frame tunnel beneath the rear seat.

The engine number is stamped on the crankcase below the generator support pedestal.

Vital Statistics

You're going to need to know a lot of the facts that follow at some time or another, whether it's for servicing purposes or just to help you win a bet in the local! Let's run through all the main specifications, starting with the engine ...

ENGINE

Type	4 cylinder, horizontally opposed flat, pushrod ohv	
Cubic capacity:	*Bore*	*Stroke*
1192 cc (1200)	77 mm	64 mm
1285 cc (1300)	77 mm	69 mm
1493 cc (1500)	83 mm	69 mm
1584 cc (1600)	85·5 mm	69 mm
Compression ratio and bhp:	*CR*	*DIN bhp at rpm*
1192 cc (up to August 1960)	6·6 : 1	30 at 3400
1192 cc (from August 1960)	7·0 : 1	34 at 3600
1192 cc (code D)	7·3 : 1	34 at 3800
1285 cc (to August 1970 code F)	7·3 : 1	40 at 4000
1285 cc (from August 1970 code AB and AR)	7·5 : 1	44 at 4100
1285 cc (low compression code AC)	6·6 : 1	40 at 4000
1493 cc (code H)	7·5 : 1	44 at 4000
1584 cc (code AD, AE, AH, AR and AS)	7·5 : 1	50 at 4000
1584 cc (low compression code AF)	6·6 : 1	46 at 4000
Torque (maximum):	*ft lbs (mkg) at rpm*	
30 DIN bhp	55·7 (7·7) at 2000	
34 DIN bhp (from August 1960)	60·76 (8·4) at 2000	
34 DIN bhp (code D)	54·97 (7·6) at 1700	
40 DIN bhp (code F)	69 (9·5) at 2600	
44 DIN bhp (code AB and AR)	63 (8·7) at 3000	
40 DIN bhp (code AC)	58 (8·0) at 3000	
44 DIN bhp (code H)	78 (10·7) at 2600	
50 DIN bhp (code AD, AE, and AS)	77 (10·6) at 2800	
46 DIN bhp (code AF)	72 (10·0) at 2600	
Firing order	1 (right front cylinder) – 4 (left rear cylinder) – 3 (left front cylinder) – 2 (right rear cylinder)	
Valve clearances:		
Pre 1960, 30 DIN bhp	0·004 in (0·1 mm) inlet and exhaust	
1960 to 1965, 34 DIN bhp	0·008 in (0·2 mm) inlet, 0·012 in (0·3 mm) exhaust	
1966 on, 34 DIN bhp (to code D)	0·004 in (0·1 mm) inlet and exhaust	
1966 on, 34 DIN bhp (code D)	0·006 in (0·15 mm) inlet and exhaust	
1300 code F, AB, AR, and AC	0·006 in (0·15 mm) inlet and exhaust	
1500 code H	0·006 in (0·15 mm) inlet and exhaust	
1600 code AD, AE, AF, AH, AR and AS	0·006 in (0·15 mm) inlet and exhaust	

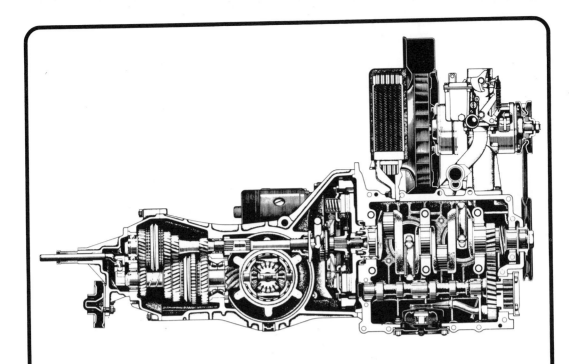

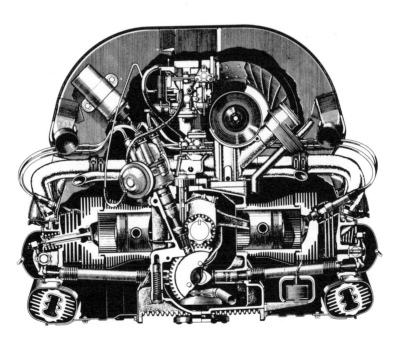

Cross-sectional views of the Beetle engine and transmission

COOLING SYSTEM

Type	Air cooled by fan and ducting
Thermostat opens at	65° to 70°C (149° to 158°F)
Fan belt free play	New – 0·4 in (10 mm); Used – 0·5 in (12 mm)

FUEL SYSTEM

Fuel pump	Mechanical – Pierburg
Air cleaner:	
Early models	Oil bath – metal body
Late models	Paper element – plastic body
Carburettor type:	
1200 engine (early)	Solex 28 PCI, 28 PCIT, 28 PCIT-1
1200 engine (later)	Solex 30 PICT-3
1300 engine	Solex 30 PICT-1, 30 PICT-2, 31 PICT-3, 31 PICT-4
1500 engine (early)	Solex 30 PICT-1, 30 PICT-2
1500 engine (later)	Solex 31 PICT-3
1600 engine	Solex 34 PICT-3, 34 PICT-4

LUBRICATION SYSTEM

Type	Wet sump – pressure and splash
Oil filter	Gauze strainer in sump
Oil pump type	Twin gear
Oil cooler type	Pressure fed multi-tube in cooling fan housing
Sump capacity:	
Initial fill	5·3 pints (3·0 litres)
Oil change	4·4 pints (2·5 litres)

IGNITION SYSTEM

Spark plugs:	
Size	14 mm thread
Type	Bosch W 175 T1, W 145 T1 (cold climates)
	Champion L10, L85, L87y, L88A (cold climates)
	KLG F70 Bem 175/14, 145/14 (cold climates)
Electrode gap:	
All models except for 1500 cc	0·024 in (0·6 mm)
1500 cc	0·028 in (0·7 mm)
Contact points gap	0·016 in (0·4 mm)
Dwell angle:	
Wear limit	42° to 58°
Normal setting	44° to 50°
Ignition timing:	
1200 cc engine (1955 to 1966)	10° BTDC
1200 cc engine (except 1955 to 1966)	7½° BTDC
1300 cc engine (engine numbers F0, 000, 001 to F2, 140, 1820 with vacuum advance only)	7½° BTDC – vacuum hose off
1300 cc engine (engine numbers ABO, 000, 001 to ABO, 313, 345 with double vacuum and centrifugal advance)	5° ATDC – vacuum hoses on
1300 cc engine (engine number ABO, 313, 346 on with vacuum advance only)	7½° BTDC – vacuum hose off, speed 850 ± 50 rpm
1500 cc engine (engine numbers HO, 204, 001 to HO, 879, 926)	7½° BTDC
1500 cc engine (engine numbers HO, 879, 927 to H1, 124, 669 fitted with automatic transmission)	0°
1500 cc engine (engine numbers H1, 124, 670 to H1, 259, 314)	7½° BTDC

© HAYNES

Cutaway view of VW Beetle 1200

Terry Dav...

1500 cc engine (remaining engine numbers in H range)

0°

1600 cc engine (engine numbers B6, 000, 001 to B6, 440, 900)

0° — vacuum hose off (manual) or on (automatic)

1600 cc engine (codes AD, AE, AF, AK and AH with double vacuum

5° ATDC — vacuum hoses on

1600 cc engine (codes AD, AK, AH, AR, and AS with single vacuum)

$7\frac{1}{2}$° BTDC — vacuum hose off

CLUTCH (MANUAL GEARBOX)

Type — Single dry plate disc, toggle release (early models) or diaphragm spring (later models)

Operation — Cable

Pedal free play — 0·4 to 1·0 in (10 to 25 mm)

GEARBOX (MANUAL)

Ratios:	1st	2nd	3rd	4th	Reverse
Split casing, non-synchro	3·60 : 1	2·07 : 1	1·25 : 1	0·80 : 1	6·60 : 1
Split casing, 3-speed synchro	3·60 : 1	1·94 or 1·88 : 1	1·23 or 1·22 : 1	0·82 : 1	4·63 : 1
1200 one piece casing (early)	3·8 : 1	2·06 : 1	1·26 : 1	0·82 or 0·89 : 1	3·88 or 3·62 : 1
1200 one piece casing (later) and late 1300	3·78 : 1	2·06 : 1	1·26 : 1	0·93 : 1	3·79 : 1
1500 and early 1300	3·80 : 1	2·06 : 1	1·26 or 1·32 : 1	0·89 : 1	3·61 or 3·88 : 1
1600 (early)	3·80 : 1	2·06 : 1	1·26 : 1	0·89 : 1	3·61 or 3·80 : 1
1600 (later)	3·78 : 1	2·06 : 1	1·26 : 1	0·93 : 1	3·79 : 1

Gearbox oil capacity (including final drive):

Initial fill — 5·3 pints (3·0 litres)

Oil change — 4·4 pints (2·5 litres)

AUTOMATIC STICK-SHIFT TRANSMISSION

Type — Conventional gearbox with clutch and torque converter

Operation — Clutch operated pneumatically by electric control

Ratios:	Low	Medium	High	Reverse
1500 and early 1300	2·06 : 1	1·26 : 1	0·89 : 1	3·07 : 1
Early 1600	2·25 : 1	1·26 : 1	0·89 : 1	3·07 : 1
1300 and 1600 (later models)	2·25 : 1	1·26 : 1	0·82 or 0·88 : 1	3·07 : 1

Torque converter capacity — 7·5 pints (3·6 litres)

FINAL DRIVE

Location — Integral with gearbox

Ratio:	Manual	Automatic
1200	4·375 : 1	—
1300	4·375 : 1	4·375 : 1
1500	4·125 : 1	4·375 : 1
1600 (early)	3·875 : 1	4·375 : 1
1600 (later)	3·875 : 1	4·125 : 1 or 4·375 : 1

BRAKING SYSTEM

Type — Hydraulically operated, drums or discs front wheels, drums rear wheels

Terry Davey

© HAYNES

Cutaway view of VW Beetle 1303

Handbrake	Cable operated to rear wheels
Minimum shoe lining thickness	0·020 in (0·5 mm) above rivet heads
Minimum pad thickness	0·079 in (2·0 mm)
Master cylinder type:	
Early models	Single port
Later models	Tandem, dual circuit

ELECTRICAL SYSTEM

Battery:	
Early 1200, 1300, and 1500	6 volt, lead acid
All later models	12 volt, lead acid
Earth	Negative
Generator	Bosch or VW dynamo, or Bosch alternator
Starter motor:	
Early models	Bosch or VW pre-engaged 6 volt, 0·5 hp
Later models	Bosch or VW pre-engaged 12 volt, 0·7 hp (manual) or 0·8 hp (automatic)
Light bulbs:	*Wattage*
Headlamp	45/40 (Normal) or 60/55 (Halogen)
Parking lamp	4
Stop/tail lamp	18/5 or 21/5
Turn indicator lamp	18 or 21, 21/5 with sealed beam headlamps
Rear number plate	10
Interior light	10 festoon (saloon), 5 festoon (convertible)
Instrument panel warning lamps	2 or 1·2
Reversing light	21

SUSPENSION

Front:	
All models except Super Beetle, 1303, and 1303S	Independent, twin transverse laminated leaf torsion bars, each with a trailing arm to the steering knuckle or link
1971 on Super Beetle models, 1303, and 1303S	Independent MacPherson struts with built-in shock absorbers and coil springs. Anti roll bar fitted
Rear:	
All models except Super Beetle, 1303, and 1303S	Independent single divided transverse solid torsion bar with trailing spring plate to outer end of swing axle tube which pivots at transmission. Separate shock absorbers.
1971 on Super Beetle models, 1303, and 1303S	Independent single divided transverse solid torsion bar with trailing link to outer end of diagonal semi-trailing arm. Double jointed driveshafts and separate shock absorbers

STEERING

Type:		
Early models (approximately pre 1960)	Worm and sector	
Later models (except 1975 1303 and 1303S)	Worm and roller	
1975 1303 and 1303S models	Rack and pinion	
Turning circle (approximate)	36 feet (11 metres)	
Front wheel geometry (unladen):	*Trailing arm*	*MacPherson strut*
Toe in (no pressure on wheels)	+ 30′ ± 15′	+ 30′ ± 15′
Camber (straight ahead position)	+ 30′ ± 20′	+ 1° + 20′ − 40′
Castor	3°20′ ± 1°	2° ± 35′

42

WHEELS AND TYRES

Type	Steel disc, 5 (early) or 4 (late) bolt fixing
Rim	4J x 15 (early), $4\frac{1}{2}$J x 15 (late), $5\frac{1}{2}$J x 15 (optional)
Tyres:	
Crossply	560–15, 4PR or 600–15L 4PR
Radial ply	155 SR 15, 165 SR 15, or 175/70 SR 15

DIMENSIONS AND WEIGHTS

Overall measurements:	
Wheelbase	94·5 in (2400 mm) – except 1302S and 1303
	95·3 in (2420 mm) – 1302S and 1303
Track (front):	
Pre-1957 models	50·5 in (1282 mm)
Later models	51·5 in (1308 mm) – drum brakes; 51·7 in
	(1314 mm) – disc brakes
Track (rear):	
Early models	50·7 in (1287 mm) – 4 bolt wheels
	53.54 in (1360 mm) – 5 bolt wheels
Later models	53·1 in (1348 mm)
Overall length (approximate):	
1200 models	160·2 in (4070 mm)
1300 models	158·6 in (4030 mm)
1500 and Super Beetle models	160·6 in (4080 mm)
Overall width (approximate):	
1200 models	61·0 in (1550 mm)
1300 models	61·0 in (1550 mm)
1500 and Super Beetle models	62·4 in (1585 mm)
Overall height (approximate):	
All models	59·0 in (1500 mm)
Ground clearance	5·9 in (150 mm)
Kerb weights (approximate):	
1200 models	1675 lbs (760 kg)
1300 models	1808 lbs (820 kg)
1500 and Super Beetle models and	1918 lbs (870 kg) – saloon; 2028 lbs (920 kg) –
convertible models	convertible
Maximum roof load	110 lbs (50 kg)
Maximum trailer weight:	
All models	1763 lbs (800 kg) with brakes; 882 lbs (400 kg)
	without brakes
Maximum trailer nose weight	55 to 110lbs (25 to 50 kg)

Tools for the Job

In *Save It!* we emphasized not only the need for regular servicing but also the money that can be saved by carrying out this work yourself. If you're tempted to have a go at servicing then you'll obviously need at the very least a basic set of tools.

The only tools supplied with the car are a wheelbrace and jack for changing a wheel in the event of a puncture. Therefore, unless you can borrow some suitable equipment, you'll need to dip into the old piggy-bank and pay a visit to your local tool or accessory shop to get the necessary items for the maintenance tasks you're likely to be undertaking.

If your piggy-bank, like most people's, isn't particularly full, then you won't want to spend any more than is absolutely necessary. Careful consideration must therefore be given to your most immediate requirements. A basic list of tools likely to be needed is given below, but remember when buying tools, that 'you gets what you pays for' and cheap tools aren't usually very good value!

It makes sense to pay a little extra to get a good quality tool which will not only last longer, but is designed correctly and is therefore better to use. It may be true that 'a bad workman always blames his tools' but at the same time bad tools don't usually make for a particularly good workman!

Although the initial outlay for tools may seem somewhat startling, remember that much of this will be repaid in the cash saved by having no garage bill for labour charges at the next full service.

It's not possible to tell you exactly what tools you'll be needing, but the lists below are intended as a general guide. As we've explained, the first list gives the basic tools required for simple service procedures. In the second list, some of the more sophisticated tools are suggested such as will be found in the average professional garage, and will widen the scope from simple maintenance tasks to the more involved repair jobs on the car.

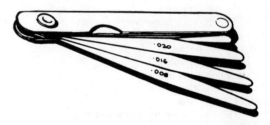

Feeler gauges

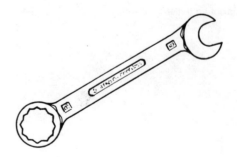

Combination ring/open-ended spanner

Adjustable spanner – 9 in approx.
Spark plug spanner (with rubber insert and cranked drive)
Set of feeler gauges
Screwdriver – 4 in blade x $\frac{1}{4}$ in diameter (plain)

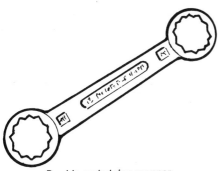

Double-ended ring spanner

Screwdriver — 4 in blade x $\frac{1}{4}$ in diameter (crosshead)
Junior hacksaw (and spare blades)
Combination spanner set – sizes 8 to 27 mm
Grease gun
Hydraulic or screw type pillar jack
Wire brush
Emery cloth
Medium size funnel
Tool box

The tools listed above should normally enable you to complete the servicing procedures detailed later in the book. Assuming that you'll be successful in this respect, we hope you'll find the various chores easier than anticipated, and possibly even attempt some other simple repair jobs as and when necessary.

If you're really keen and intend attempting some of the more involved repairs, you'll need to invest in a more comprehensive tool kit. Another essential requirement will be the Haynes Owners Workshop Manual which explains just about everything you'll need to know to repair or overhaul the various components of your Beetle. In addition to the tools listed above, the following will enable you to attempt the more serious repair and maintenance jobs:

Steel ramp

Socket set (metric), with $\frac{1}{2}''$ drive and with a reversible ratchet, extension bar, universal joint and T-bar
An engineer's hammer (ball pein) – 1 lb
Soft head mallet (copper/hide)
Pair of pliers
Wire strippers
A combination screwdriver set (with flat and crossheads included)
Axle stands
Ramps
Vice
G-clamps
Set of metal files
Hacksaw (and spare blades)
Hand and/or power drill

Other more specialised tools, such as circlip pliers or ring compressors, can be purchased, hired or borrowed as and when required which hopefully, won't be too often!

You'll also need a container to drain the old oil into; an old washing-up bowl is ideal, or alternatively, old 1 gallon (5 litre) oil cans are suitable if you cut a hole in the side face.

Most people dislike getting dirty, and therefore a pair of overalls will be needed to keep you recognisable! Finally, it's a good idea to have some handcleaner, which will make light work of removing **45**

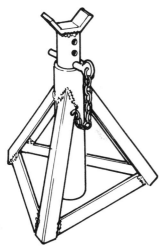

Axle stand

grease and grime from your skin.

While we're talking about tools, it's worth mentioning some of the tune-up aids that are on the market. A visit to a good motor accessory shop can be an enlightening experience, just to show you the sort of things available. Later in this book, you'll find a bit about 'bolt-on-goodies', but all we'll concern ourselves with here are three items.

Stroboscopic timing light

The most accurate way of checking ignition timing (that's the time at which the spark occurs) is with the engine running, and for this a stroboscopic (strobe) light is used. This is connected to No. 1 spark plug lead and the beam is shone on to the crankshaft pulley mark. Any proprietary light is supplied with full connecting and operating instructions.

Dwell angle meter

This is used for measuring the period of time for which the distributor points remain closed during the ignition cycle of one cylinder, and provides a more accurate method of setting-up the points gap. Dwell angle meters normally incorporate a tachometer (rev counter if you prefer), which can be useful for checking engine idle speed.

Cylinder compression gauge

This is very useful for tracing the cause of a fall-off in engine performance. It consists of a pressure gauge and non-return valve, and is simply screwed into a spark plug hole while the engine is turned over on the starter.

Two other useful items are a hydrometer, which is used for checking the specific gravity of the battery electrolyte (this will tell you if you have a dud cell which won't hold a charge), and a 6 or 12 volt (according to model) lamp on an extension lead with crocodile clips which can be connected to the battery terminals.

Tool care

Having spent time and money in acquiring a tool kit, it's obviously to your advantage to look after it. Collect the various tools together after use and wipe them clean – don't leave them lying around

Items such as screwdrivers, files and pliers can be easily located out of the way in a simple rack on the garage wall. Spanners are probably best kept in a metal tool box.

Socket sets are another expensive item that must be looked after. Check that all the sockets used are replaced in the container. The moulded trays for the various sockets are usually made in plastic these days, and are therefore comparatively fragile. Once the plastic breaks, it's easy for the sockets to be mixed up and misplaced, so handle this with care.

Delicate tools such as gauges and meters should also be handled with care and stored in a safe place to avoid damage. Don't use damaged or broken tools – renew them.

Service Scene

In the previous chapters we've considered some of the main facts about the Beetle range, but now's the time to get down to the servicing and maintenance tasks, which is where you're really going to be able to save some money.

Before long you'll realise that your Beetle is quite simply constructed, and given proper maintenance will serve you well. It doesn't require a vast amount of time, money or technical knowledge to service it, so we're going to set out the procedures for the various maintenance tasks necessary.

Obviously a basic tool kit will be necessary for most of these service procedures, and some information on tool requirements is given in *Tools for the Job.*

In addition to tools, certain items will be required before commencing the relevant service, such as oil, grease, air filter etc, as specified at the beginning of the Schedule concerned.

A suitable work area in which to carry out the various tasks must also be found. People with their own garage will not have this problem, but those who don't should choose a flat piece of ground on which to work and make sure that it doesn't block anyone's right of way. Remember, when working you may find that a component requires repairing or renewing, in which case the car may have to be left in the work area for an extended period in a partly dismantled state.

We've tried to present the servicing tasks in a logical way to minimize the amount of jacking up etc, which may be a prelude to the actual job. The items listed are basically those recommended by the car manufacturer, but are supplemented by some additional ones which we think are well worth the extra trouble.

If you've recently bought the car, the safest thing is to go right through all the Service Schedules, unless you can really satisfy yourself that the previous owner was as meticulous about things as you'd like to be. If you don't use the car regularly, and aren't likely to clock up the mileage until well after the time interval, *always* use the time interval as the basis for servicing.

You'll notice that there are Spring and Autumn schedules too, just so that you can make sure the car's in the best possible state for the season ahead.

Certain adverse operating conditions will affect the engine oil change mileage. If you only use your car for short journeys or consistent stop-start operation, or in extremes of cold or heat, you should reduce your oil change mileage from the normal 3000 miles. Similarly when driving regularly in very dusty conditions it will be necessary to change the air cleaner element more often.

Safety

Accidents do happen, but 99% of them can be prevented by taking a little care. We're going to list a few points which should reduce any accident risk, and we'd like you to read through them before starting work – it could prove to be very worthwhile.

DON'T run the engine in the garage with the doors closed.

DON'T work in an inspection pit with the engine running – the fumes will tend to concentrate at the lowest point.

DO keep long hair, sleeves, ties and the like well clear of any rotating parts when the engine's running.

DON'T grab hold of ignition HT leads when the engine's running – there's just the possibility of an electric shock, particularly if the leads are dirty or wet.

DO chock the rear wheels when jacking up the front of the car, and vice versa. Where possible, also apply the handbrake and engage first or reverse gear.

DON'T rely on the car jack when you're working underneath. Axle stands, or wooden or concrete blocks should be used, but choose the points of support sensibly to prevent damaging anything. **47**

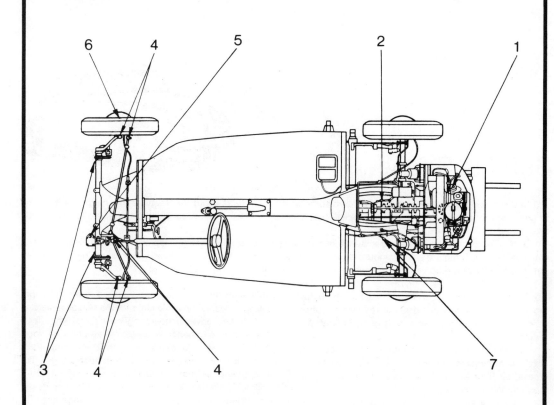

Lubrication chart

1	Engine	SAE 20W/50 multigrade engine oil
2	Transmission	SAE 90 EP gear oil
	Torque converter (semi-automatic transmission)	Dexron type automatic transmission fluid
3	Front axle tubes (2 nipples each side)	General purpose lithium-based grease
4	King pins (2 nipples each side) and balljoints (4 nipples)	General purpose lithium-based grease
5	Steering gear-early models only	SAE 90EP gear oil
6	Front wheel bearings	General purpose lithium-based grease
7	Handbrake cables – early models only (one nipple each side)	General purpose lithium-based grease
–	Oil bath air cleaner	SAE 20W/50 multigrade engine oil
–	Brake fluid reservoir	SAE J1 703 hydraulic fluid

Note: The above are general recommendations only. The chart illustrates a typical model in the Beetle range, but details on your car may vary. If in doubt, refer to Service Scene *and* Vital Statistics.

DO wipe up grease or oil from the floor if you spill any (and you will do, sooner or later).

DO get someone to check regularly that everything's OK if you're likely to be spending some time underneath the car.

DON'T use a file or similar tool without a handle. The tang can give you a nasty gash if something goes wrong.

DO make sure when you're using a spanner, that it's the right size for the nut and that it's properly fitted before tightening or loosening.

DO brush away any drilling swarf with an old paintbrush – never your fingers.

DON'T allow battery acid or battery terminal corrosion to contact the skin or clothes. If it should happen, wash off immediately with plenty of cold running water.

DON'T rush any job – that's how mistakes are made. If you don't think you'll finish the job in time, do it tomorrow, but try not to make this an excuse for forgetting about it.

DO take care when pouring brake fluid. If it spills on the paintwork and isn't removed immediately, it'll take the paint off. And wash your hands well afterwards as it's poisonous.

SERVICE SCHEDULES
WEEKLY, BEFORE A LONG JOURNEY, OR EVERY 250 MILES (450 KM)

The following tools, lubricants, etc are likely to be needed:

Tyre pressure gauge, wheel nut spanner, lint-free cloth, engine oil, distilled water, hydraulic brake fluid.

1   Check engine oil level (car on level ground)

The engine oil level is best checked when the engine's cold. If it's just been running, wait a minute or two for the oil to drain back into the 'sump' then pull the dipstick up and out. Wipe it clean on a lint-free cloth then fully insert it back into the engine; now pull it out again and check the level. Add oil if necessary to bring it up to the top mark on the dipstick.

Never overfill the engine with oil; not only is it wasteful but it can also finds its way out of an overloaded oil seal. Take care when pouring oil in through the filler neck; the best method is to use a funnel.

When you're satisfied the job's completed, ensure that the dipstick and filler cap are properly fitted, then wipe away any oil which may have been spilt.

2   Check battery electrolyte level

Lift out the rear seat cushion being careful not to damage the backrest, then wipe away any dirt or·

moisture from the top of the battery so that none can get inside. Remove the caps or cover from the battery cells and check the electrolyte level (with some makes of battery, the case is made of translucent material and the electrolyte level can be seen through it). Add distilled water to bring the level to just above the tops of the battery plates; on some types of battery (eg Lucas Pacemaker) distilled water's added to the trough until all the rectangular filling slots are full and the bottom of the trough's just covered. If for some reason you don't have any distilled water (and it does happen) you can use the frost which collects on the walls of your freezer or fridge and allow this to melt. If you're really stuck, and as a last resort, boil up some water in a kettle and allow it to cool, but don't make a habit of it or the battery will suffer in the long run.

Refit the cell caps or battery cover, carefully wiping away any drops of water that were spilt, then check that the terminals are tight. A very light smear of petroleum jelly can be applied to prevent any corrosion from getting a foothold. If the weather's extremely cold, run the engine for a few minutes; this will charge the battery and mix the electrolyte which will prevent the added water from freezing.

3   Top up windscreen washer reservoir

Where this is fitted it's located in the front luggage compartment, but depending on the model the reservoir will be positioned either in the spare wheel or on a side panel. Air pressure from the spare wheel is used to force the water through the jets and a special valve ensures that the spare wheel pressure never drops below about 28 psi. If the washer refuses to work it's worthwhile checking that there's sufficient pressure in the spare wheel. To top up the water level, remove the filler cap and add soft water together with a little proprietary detergent until it overflows. To prevent the water freezing in cold weather, methylated spirit (3 to 1 proportion) or a special antifreeze sachet can be added but **don't** use ordinary radiator antifreeze. Finally check that the screen jets operate correctly.

4   Check tyre pressures and tread condition

With the tyres cold, check the pressures (see *Filling Station Facts*). If possible, use your own gauge – those on garage forecourts tend to be abused and inaccurate. Don't forget the spare wheel; the pressure here should be up to the maximum ever likely to be needed – letting some air out is much easier than blowing it up if the wheel has to be used in an emergency.

With the tyres correctly inflated, run your hands and eyes over the tyre walls and tread. This is best done with the wheel off the ground so that it can be **49** rotated but, if you're really not feeling up to it, move the car backwards or forwards a foot or so, so that you can check all round. If you have a tyre tread depth gauge, check that the tread is at least 1 mm deep throughout at least threequarters of the tyre width. Alternatively a 2p piece can be used as a rough guide. Insert the coin into the tread and, if it's not deeper than the distance from the row of dots to the edge of the coin, you're breaking the law so get some replacements pretty quickly! There must be no cuts, bulges or other deformities; if these are present, you're breaking the law again.

If you've got to buy new tyres, read the bit in *Save It* but remember that it's illegal to drive with a crossply and a radial ply on the same end of the car. The only permissible combination is crossplies on the front and radials on the rear but, think of the problem you'll have if you get a puncture. For safety's sake use a complete set of tyres of the same type.

5 Check tightness of wheel nuts

While you're down at floor level, it's a good time to check the tightness of the wheel nuts. Remove the hub cap or plastic wheel nut covers (where applicable) and just check that the wheel nuts are tight, using the wheelbrace which should be with your jack. There's no need to stand on the wheelbrace because someday the wheel will have to come off again, but the nuts should be tightened firmly. Finally don't forget to refit the hub cap or wheel nut covers (only where applicable).

6 Check the brake fluid level

The brake fluid reservoir's located in the front luggage compartment on the left-hand side and on later models it's possible to check the fluid level without removing the cap. If there's no level marking, to correct level is at the plastic ridge.

Before removing the filler cap, clean it and the surrounding area with a lint-free cloth. This will stop any unwanted material getting into the braking system. Use only genuine brake fluid for topping up the level and remember not to overfill the reservoir. Brake fluid's highly corrosive and will ruin any paintwork it comes in contact with, so don't spill any.

If the fluid level falls frequently, you most probably have a leak which means trouble, so investigate and rectify the fault immediately. However, especially with disc brakes, the level tends to sink slightly as the pad wear is taken up by the automatic adjustment and this is quite normal.

7 Check that all the lights work

Switch on the car lights and check that everything works correctly. If a bulb needs renewing, refer to *In an Emergency* for details.

Checking battery electrolyte level

Windscreen washer reservoir location (some models)

Brake fluid reservoir location

Engine oil drain plug located in centre of filter cover

Component parts of the engine oil filter screen

Dismantling the generator pulley

8   Relax

You've successfully completed the first of the regular service routines!

EVERY 3000 MILES (5000 KM) OR 3 MONTHS, WHICHEVER COMES FIRST
(In addition to the checks detailed in the Weekly/250 mile Schedule)

The following tools, lubricants etc, are likely to be needed:

Drain plug spanner, container, engine oil, filter gaskets, assorted metric spanners, plug spanner, feeler gauges, emery tape, timing light or lamp, screwdriver, paraffin, gearbox plug key, disc pads, grease gun, oil can, glycerine.

1   Change engine oil and clean oil filter screen

Note: *Under certain adverse operating conditions such as repeated stop/start driving or driving in extremely hot or cold conditions, it is advisable to reduce the engine oil change interval to 1500 miles and even 750 miles in arctic conditions.*

Oil changes should only be made with the engine warm as this allows the oil to drain out easier. So if it's not warm, drive around for a mile or two – this is better than leaving a cold engine idling because less wear will take place.

Now get a suitable container (at least 5 pints – 2.84 litres capacity) which will fit under the engine. A plastic washing-up bowl is the sort of thing that will do the job nicely.

Now prepare yourself for the dirty part! Lie on the ground and remove the drain plug if fitted; you can use the spark plug spanner if you like. If on later models the drain plug's not fitted you'll have to remove five of the strainer plate retaining nuts and just loosen the sixth one. Be prepared to get oil on your fingers, and possibly all over your hand, so do it as quickly as possible. If by chance you've dropped the drain plug into the container, don't forget it's there – you're going to need it later on.

When most of the oil has drained, the oil strainer must be removed and cleaned, and this should be done at every oil change interval. Unscrew all of the cover retaining nuts and remove the copper washers, then use a screwdriver to prise the cover and strainer from the crankcase. Separate the strainer from the plate, then remove all traces of gasket including any which may be on the crankcase surface. Thoroughly clean the strainer and plate in paraffin or petrol then wipe the gasket contact surfaces dry with a lint-free cloth.

By now all of the oil should have drained from the engine, so wipe the crankcase dry. Place a gasket each side of the strainer flange and put this on the **51**

Generator pulley adjustment shim locations

belt because, if it's cracked or split it must be renewed anyway.

Adjustment is made by varying the number of the shims between the generator split pulley halves, so if you only need to adjust the belt, you'll have to note how many shims are positioned there in the first place. By removing shims the belt tension is increased and by adding extra shims the tension is decreased.

To remove the fan belt, unscrew the nut and remove the clamp ring from the generator pulley shaft; at the same time lock the inner pulley with a screwdriver in the slot and notch provided. Remove the outer spare shims followed by the outer pulley shaft and inner shims. The fan belt can now be removed from the crankshaft pulley although on some later models it may be necessary to remove a collar first.

Fit the new fan belt on the crankshaft pulley and refit the collar where necessary. Hold the upper part of the fan belt against the generator inner pulley half and refit the inner spacer shims, outer pulley half, outer shims and clamp ring, and nut. Use a screwdriver in the inner pulley half slot to hold the pulley still whilst tightening the nut, and occasionally allow the pulley to rotate in order to settle the fan belt. When the nut is really tight, check the tension as previously described. If adjustment is necessary, the generator pulley must be dismantled again and the quantity of shims altered as necessary. Always make sure that the spare shims are fitted to the outside of the pulley and not just left out altogether. Incidentally, the nut on the generator can be loosened with the spark plug spanner; a point worth noting if you're broken down without a tool kit.

3   Clean the spark plugs

These are slightly awkward to locate and a spark plug spanner is a must together with a 90° tommy bar or cranked socket drive. First pull off the plug caps, and if you think you won't know where each one goes when you put them back, a dab of paint on the cable or plug cap will identify them. Remember that the cylinders are numbered 1 and 2, front and rear on the right-hand side, and 3 and 4, front and rear on the left-hand side if you want to mark the plug caps with their correct numbers. Brush any dirt from around the plug bodies to prevent it falling into the engine, then remove each plug using the plug spanner. The plugs should ideally be cleaned by a garage equipped with a sand-blasting machine, which will remove the deposits far more effectively than using a wire brush. A spare set of plugs overcomes the inconvenience of having to walk to the garage and in this way you'll always have a spare set ready to use.

cover plate, then locate everything over the studs in the bottom of the crankcase. If the old copper washers are still serviceable they can be used again; if not fit new washers. Screw on the retaining nuts and tighten them evenly in diagonal sequence but not too tight or the threads may give way. Screw in the drain plug where fitted together with a new copper washer if necessary and tighten it with the plug spanner.

Now add the new engine oil until the level is up to the top mark on the dipstick. Run the engine and check that there are no leaks from the strainer plate, then stop the engine and recheck the oil level after five minutes.

There's always a problem with disposing of waste oil, but if you buy it in 5-litre cans you can put the old oil in them and let the dustman take them away. Some garages will take the old oil off your hands but one thing you must not do is to pour it down the household drain; it's illegal as well as anti-social.

2   Check fan belt

Failure of the fan belt on the VW engine means that you're left with no battery charging and no engine cooling; so it pays to make a really thorough check when the time comes; it also pays to carry a spare belt around with you in the luggage compartment.

To check the fan belt tension, press your thumb firmly against the belt at a point midway between the generator and crankshaft pulleys; the belt should deflect by the amount given in *Vital Statistics*. If the tension is not right, first check the condition of the

Checking plug gap with feeler gauges

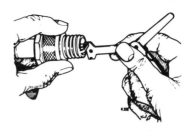

Altering the plug gap. Note use of correct tool

Spark plug maintenance

White deposits and damaged porcelain insulation indicating overheating

Broken porcelain insulation due to bent central electrode

Electrodes burnt away due to wrong heat value or chronic pre-ignition (pinking)

Excessive black deposits caused by over-rich mixture or wrong heat value

Mild white deposits and electrode burnt indicating too weak a fuel mixture

Plug in sound condition with light greyish brown deposits

Spark plug electrode conditions

53

Wipe the plug insulators with a petrol moistened cloth, and check that the screw thread's clean. Check the electrode gap using a feeler gauge of the correct thickness, and if necessary bend the outer electrode to obtain it. Never try to bend the central electrode – all you'll achieve is a broken insulator.

When the plugs are clean and reset, check that the seating in the cylinder head is clean and the seating washer's on the plug. Apply a few drops of oil to the plug threads then tighten them down firmly – but no white knuckles or bulging cheeks, you've got to get them out again one day! Don't bother to fit the plug leads yet, because you'll need them off for the next item ...

4 Clean contact breaker points and lubricate distributor

After a period of time, due to the sparking which occurs across them, the contact points will need cleaning. A build-up occurs on one contact and a small crater appears on the other one. When this happens, starting problems occur and there's a general fall-off of efficiency in the ignition system.

To clean the contacts, first release the two clips securing the distributor cap to the body and lift away the cap. Pull off the rotor arm and on later models remove the plastic dust cover. Early types of contact breaker points came in two separate parts with separate insulating washers, but unless your car's been laid up for some time you've probably got the later type which cannot be dismantled. Either way unscrew the retaining screw and put it in a safe place, then disconnect the low tension wire at the terminal On early models a small screw and nut secured the wire, whereas on later models a clip was fitted. The complete contact points can now be lifted from the distributor.

To reface the contacts, rub them on a fine carborundum stone or a piece of fine emery cloth, but make sure that both points are kept square and smooth so that they'll make good contact when refitted. Clean the abrasive away with methylated spirit, then refit the contact points to the distributor pivot post. Reconnect the terminal wire and insert the retaining screw but don't tighten it yet.

Using the plug spanner on the generator nut, turn the engine until the heel of the moving contact rests on the highest point of one of the four cam lobes. Now out with the feeler gauges again and select the size given in *Vital Statistics* for the points gap. Place the feeler between the contact faces and adjust the gap by moving the fixed point plate either way as necessary. Use a screwdriver blade in the notch provided to make a fine adjustment and, when the feeler blade slides firmly between the two contacts

54 without forcing them apart, tighten the retaining

Checking the fan belt tension

Removing a spark plug

Distributor showing contact breaker points

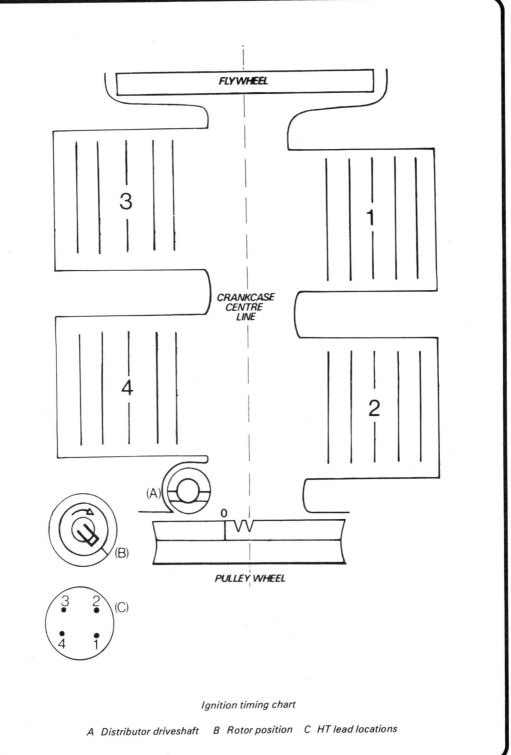

FLYWHEEL

3

1

CRANKCASE
CENTRE
LINE

4

2

(A)

(B)

0

3 2 (C)

4 1

PULLEY WHEEL

Ignition timing chart

A Distributor driveshaft   B Rotor position   C HT lead locations

screw and recheck the gap. To make allowances for an eccentric distributor cam it's worth turning the engine and checking the gap on the three remaining cam lobes.

Now apply a few drops of oil to the centre of the cam spindle and allow a few drops to flow past the base of the cam to lubricate the automatic advance and retard mechanism. Lubricate the contact breaker pivot pin with a tiny spot of oil. Don't overdo this lubrication bit, as excess oil can be thrown onto the contacts causing misfiring. Smear a trace of grease on to the cam lobes to lubricate the moving point heel.

Wipe the distributor cap and plastic dust cover if fitted and check that there are no signs of tracking on the cap indicated by a thin black line between segments. Similarly wipe the plug leads and plug caps. If there's any doubt about the serviceability of these items it's best to renew them.

Refit the plastic dust cover, rotor arm, and distributor cap and push the HT lead caps firmly on the plug terminals. If you have any doubt as to the correct location of the plug leads refer to the accompanying illustration.

5   Check ignition timing

As the contact breaker heel wears or after a new contact set's been fitted, the ignition timing should be checked and adjusted. Checking the timing statically (that's with the engine stopped) is easily done and we're going to describe this method first. If you want a more accurate setting, use a stroboscope timing light and skip the first part of this section.

Remove the distributor cap and turn the engine until the rotor arm is pointing towards the notch in the distributor base; this indicates that number 1 piston in the right-hand front cylinder is at the end of its compression stroke and ready to fire the air/fuel mixture in the combustion chamber. To verify the engine position you can remove number 1 spark plug and place a finger over the plug hole while turning the engine; when the compression stops, the piston has finished the compression stroke. The timing marks on the crankshaft pulley should now be somewhere near the crankcase centre line. Refer to *Vital Statistics* and determine the correct timing position for your car, then set the notch on the pulley exactly in line with the crankcase centre line. If you have two notches then the right-hand one indicates 10.5° advance and the left-hand one 7.5° advance, if there's just one notch then that's the correct position for your engine. The line on the pulley indicates top dead centre (TDC) which is when number 1 piston is exactly at the top of its stroke.

Now take a look at the contact breaker points – they should be just opening. To make sure that

they're just opening you'll need a 6 or 12 volt test lamp (depending on your model) and leads. Connect one of the leads to the coil terminal which leads to the distributor with the existing lead still connected, then connect the remaining lead to some part of the engine to act as the earth. Loosen the distributor body clamp and turn the distributor clockwise a little so that the contact points close, then switch on the ignition and carefully turn the distributor anticlockwise until the timing light comes on. At this point the ignition timing's correct provided the timing marks on the crankshaft pulley are still in line. Tighten the clamp and check the timing again after rotating the engine two complete turns. The distributor cap can now be refitted and the timing light removed.

If you're using a stroboscopic timing light, there's no need to remove the distributor cap, just connect it up in accordance with the manufacturer's instructions. Start the engine and shine the light on the crankshaft pulley and crankcase timing marks. With the engine idling the correct timing marks should appear in line with each other, but if they're not, loosen the distributor clamp and turn the distributor until they are, then tighten the clamp. If you have a neon type timing light use chalk or paint to highlight the timing marks.

6   Clean air filter

If your car has a metal oil bath type air cleaner, first release the clips and left off the top cover. Loosen the clip at the base of the air cleaner and disconnect the strap where fitted, then detach the air heater and crankcase breather hoses. Lift the air cleaner away and empty the old oil. Clean the air cleaner thoroughly with paraffin making sure that all the sludge is removed, then wipe it dry. If the gasket between the upper and lower sections is deteriorated it should be renewed. The air flaps should also be checked for free movement and lubricated sparingly with clean engine oil.

After refitting the base of the air cleaner, fill it with clean engine oil to the level mark or step, and clip the cover in position.

If your car has a plastic paper element type air cleaner, first detach the small hoses, noting their locations. Loosen the clip and detach the air inlet hose then remove the screw which retains the support strap. Lift the air cleaner away and release the spring clips, then remove the cover and the air cleaner element. Tap the paper element to remove any accumulated dirt and dust, then wipe the air cleaner case clean with a lint-free cloth. Check that the air flaps are free to move and lubricate them sparingly.

To refit the air cleaner place the filter into the case but this time reverse its position. Clip the case

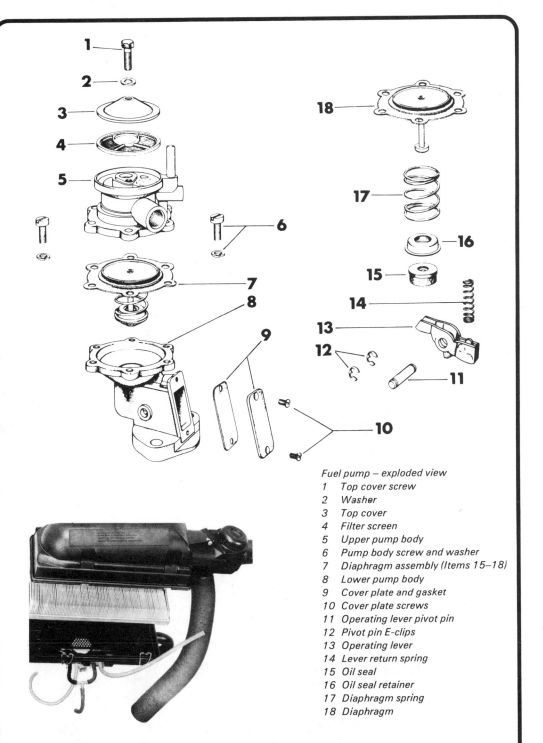

Fuel pump – exploded view
1 Top cover screw
2 Washer
3 Top cover
4 Filter screen
5 Upper pump body
6 Pump body screw and washer
7 Diaphragm assembly (Items 15–18)
8 Lower pump body
9 Cover plate and gasket
10 Cover plate screws
11 Operating lever pivot pin
12 Pivot pin E-clips
13 Operating lever
14 Lever return spring
15 Oil seal
16 Oil seal retainer
17 Diaphragm spring
18 Diaphragm

Exploded view of later type air cleaner

together and fit it to the carburettor, making sure that all the hoses are in their correct positions.

7   Clean fuel pump filter

The fuel pump's located next to the generator and two types are fitted in the Beetle range. The early type has a screw located in the centre of the cover and access to the filter is simply made by removing the screw, washer, and cover. Lift the filter gauze out and clean away any sediment by rinsing it in clean fuel and blowing through it. Clear any sediment from the pump body with a small brush and wipe it dry with a lint-free cloth. Make sure that the cover gasket is still serviceable, then refit the cover and tighten the retaining screw, but not too tight or the thread in the body will strip.

With the later type of fuel pump, unscrew the plug from the rear of the body, remove the filter and refit the plug temporarily to prevent the fuel leaking. Wash the filter in clean fuel and blow it dry, then refit it to the pump. Check that the plug washer is serviceable then tighten the plug into position.

8   Check exhaust system

Visually examine the exhaust system for deterioration and check that all the retaining nuts and bolts are secure. Start the engine and rev it several times while observing the exhaust system; this will make any leaks easier to locate.

If you do find a leak it may be possible to have it welded provided it's not too large a hole. Otherwise, the system must be renewed.

Dismantling the oil bath type air cleaner

Removing the pad retaining pin (early type)

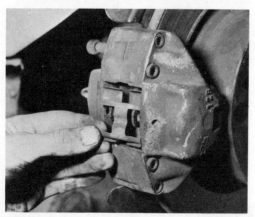

Removing the pad spring retainer plate (early type)

Removing a disc pad (early type)

9 Check the transmission and final drive oil level

You'll have to get under the car for this check and you'll also need a 17 mm hexagon Allen key to remove the level plug. Stand the car on level ground and locate the level plug on the left-hand side of the transmission casing just in front of the driveshaft. Clean the area around the plug then unscrew it and use your finger to check that the oil level is up to the bottom edge of the hole. If necessary top up the oil with the correct grade using an oil gun or squeeze pack. Before refitting the plug wait a few minutes to make doubly sure that the level's correct, otherwise you may end up with a leaking transmission oil seal.

If your car has semi-automatic transmission the level plug's on the same side of the casing as the manual version.

10 Check automatic transmission torque converter fluid level

The dipstick's located in the engine compartment on the right-hand side. Remove the dipstick and wipe it with a lint-free cloth, then fully insert it into the filler neck. Remove it again and check that the level's between the two marks. If necessary, top up the level with the correct type of fluid by pouring it directly into the dipstick tube. If you find that the level's dropped considerably, take your car to a VW agent and have it checked, otherwise you may have an expensive repair on your hands.

11 Check front brake disc pads for wear

On some later models fitted with a single disc pad retaining pin bent double, it's possible to check the pad thickness without removing the wheels, but you'll need the special VW tool. All you do is to insert the tool through the slots in the pad retaining spring towards the centre. The amount of play between the tool and the pad backing plate indicates the thickness of the pad lining, but if you can't insert the tool then it's time to renew the pads.

With the earlier type of disc pad arrangement you'll have to jack up the front of the car and remove the front wheels. Using a torchlight check that there's at least 2 mm of lining left on each pad; use a feeler gauge with long blades to make the check.

If the pads need renewing proceed as follows. On the later type jack up the front of the car and support it on axle stands, then remove the wheels. Using a pair of pliers pull the small spring clip out of the retaining pin then pull the retaining pin fork out of the brake caliper. Lift out the disc pad retaining spring noting which way round it's fitted. Unscrew the caliper retaining nuts (**not** the ones that hold the two halves together), pull the caliper from the disc, and suspend it with a length of wire. The pads can now be

removed after turning them through 90° one at a time. Move the noise damping plates to the centre of the caliper then take them out. Brush any dirt and dust from the caliper and pistons and wipe the damping plates clean. Now put the damping plates back in the caliper with the cut-out arrows facing the direction of the disc rotation (that's going forward of course). Insert the new disc pads and turn them through 90° into their correct locations. You'll have to press the pads against the pistons before the caliper can be refitted over the disc, and if this proves difficult use a small G-clamp. Normally this action will not cause the brake fluid reservoir to overflow provided the level's not too high. However, it's worthwhile checking the level after depressing each piston. If necessary use a pipette to remove some of the hydraulic fluid. Bolt the caliper onto the steering knuckle then refit the spring, fork and clip. Finally refit the wheel.

If your car's got the earlier type disc arrangement, jack up the front of the car, support it and remove the wheels. Using a parallel pin punch, drive out the retaining pin or pins from the caliper and lift away the spring plate. The pads are usually quite hard to remove and it'll therefore help if you force them away a little from the disc using a flat metal lever. Each pad can now be pulled from the caliper, but if they prove to be seized, moving them side to side and up and down several times should help. Remove the piston retaining plates noting their location. Brush away any dirt and dust from inside the caliper and pistons, but be careful not to rotate the pistons as they have a cut-away section in which the retaining plate locates. Refit the retaining plates then insert the new pads; if necessary force the pistons back into the caliper to provide the extra room for the new linings. Watch the hydraulic fluid level when doing this and remove some with a pipette if necessary. Refit the pad retaining spring then tap the retaining pin or pins into the caliper. New springs are usually provided with the new pads and where these have a narrow and a wide end, the wide end should be fitted uppermost.

With the disc pads in the calipers and the wheels refitted, pump the brake pedal several times to reposition the pistons then check the hydraulic fluid level as described earlier in this chapter.

12 Adjust the brakes

On some late models it's not possible to adjust the brakes as this is done automatically, disc brakes being fitted to the front and self adjusting brakes to the rear. You'll know if you've got the fully automatic type because there are no adjustment holes in the rear brake backplates.

To adjust the front drum type brakes, jack up the front of the car and remove the wheel caps. You'll see

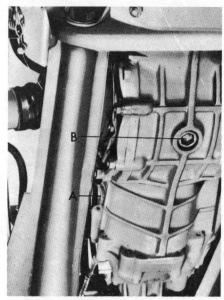

Manual gearbox filler and level plug (A), and drain plug (B)

Checking pad wear with special tool (later type)

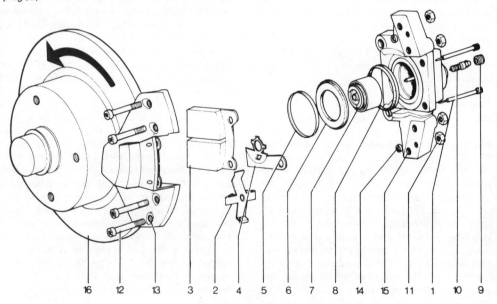

Disc and caliper components (early type)

1	Pad retaining pin	5	Clamp ring	9	Dust cap
2	Spreader spring	6	Seal	10	Bleeder valve
3	Friction pad	7	Piston	11	Hexagon nut
4	Piston retaining plate	8	Rubber seal	12	Cheese head screw

13	Caliper outer housing (assembled)
14	Seal
15	Caliper inner housing
16	Brake disc

Note: Arrow shows forward rotation of disc. Later models have modified spreader springs and only 1 retaining pin

Removing a later type disc pad

FRONT and REAR

Brake adjuster movement to lock shoes (later models)

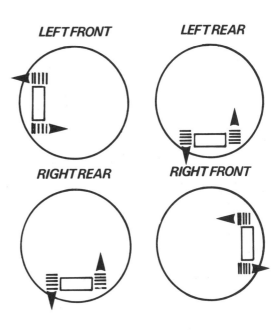

Brake adjuster movement to lock shoes (early models)

a hole through the wheel and brake drum, and by rotating the wheel slowly you'll be able to locate the adjusting ratchets. Depending on the model the adjusters are located at the front or bottom of the backplate. Using a medium size screwdriver rotate one of the adjusters until the wheel is locked, then back it off until the wheel moves freely; maybe two or three notches. Repeat the procedure on the remaining adjuster, in accordance with the accompanying illustrations, then refit the wheel cap.

Adjustment of the rear brakes is very similar to that of the front, but the adjusters are located at the bottom of the backplate and access is gained through the backplate from beneath the car. Remove the rubber plugs and turn each adjuster in turn with reference to the accompanying illustrations. Make sure that the handbrake is fully released before making the adjustment and remember that you'll feel a certain amount of transmission drag when you turn the rear wheels so don't confuse this with binding brake shoes.

If you find that a brake shoe still binds a little after backing it off three notches, leave the adjustment as it is, provided it's only superficial binding. However, if it's quite severe binding, you'll have to investigate by removing the drum, but more of this in the 6000 mile schedule.

With all the brake shoes adjusted, depress the footbrake several times and apply the handbrake three notches. Pull the cover from the handbrake lever and loosen the two cable locknuts. Now tighten each cable adjustment until each rear wheel can only just be rotated by hand, then apply the handbrake lever a further one notch and check that the rear wheels are locked solid. Tighten the cable locknuts and refit the lever cover.

13 Check the clutch adjustment
Manual transmission
The clutch pedal free play is the indicating factor to the condition of the clutch, and normally there should be 10 to 25 mm (0.4 to 1.0 in) of free play. **61**

Check this by moving the clutch pedal to and fro between the stop and the point where resistance is felt. If adjustment is needed, jack up the rear of the car and support it on axle stands. On the rear left-hand side of the gearbox you'll find a lever with a cable attached; this is the clutch release cable and the adjuster is in the form of a nut and locknut on early models and a wingnut on later models. After adjusting the cable, operate the clutch pedal several times and recheck the free play. With the wingnut type adjustment, make sure that the two lugs are engaged correctly with the lever cut-outs.

Semi-automatic transmission

You'll have to jack up the rear of the car and support it on axle stands. Locate the clutch vacuum servo on the rear left-hand side of the transmission casing and pull off the vacuum hose. Measure the distance between the bottom of the adjuster sleeve and the upper edge of the servo mounting bracket. If this is more than 4.0 mm (0.157 in), loosen the adjuster sleeve locknut and turn the sleeve away from the locknut 6.5 mm (0.256 in). Tighten the locknut against the sleeve and refit the vacuum hose. If you find that the lever touches the clutch housing as a result of adjusting it, the clutch plate is worn and should be renewed by your VW garage.

You may also adjust the clutch engagement time to suit your driving. Normally if you change from 2 to 1 at about 45 mph (72 kph) without depressing the accelerator pedal, there should be a delay of about 1 second before the drive is fully taken up. To make an adjustment, remove the cap from the top of the control valve and turn the adjustment screw in a quarter to half a turn to decrease the engagement speed, or out a quarter to half a turn to increase the engagement speed.

14 Adjust front wheel bearings

Jack up the front of the car and support it on axle stands. Now grip the top and bottom of each wheel in turn and try to rock it in and out alternately. If there's any free play noticeable the wheel bearings needs adjusting. To do this, first remove the hub cap by carefully tapping it side to side with a small hammer. On the left-hand side wheel you'll have to remove the split pin or circlip which retains the speedometer cable. On early models the adjustment is made by loosening the locknut after bending back the locktab, then turning the inner adjustment nut. On later models you'll need an Allen key to release the slotted adjusting nut.

Tighten the adjusting nut fully while rotating the wheel to start with, then loosen it and retighten it until the thrust washer just beneath the nut can just be moved by pressing on it with a screwdriver. With the adjusting nut in this position tighten the locknut

Clutch pedal free play checking point

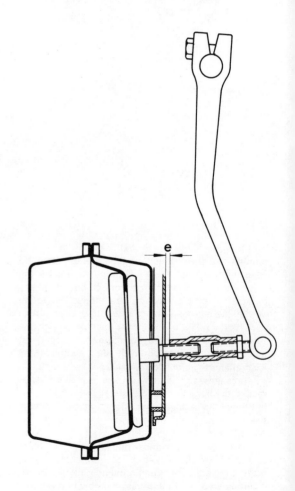

Automatic transmission checking dimension (e)

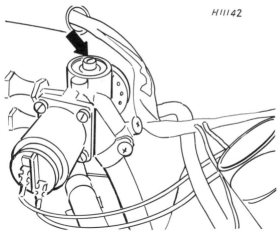

H11142

Automatic transmission control valve adjustment (arrowed)

Exploded view of front drum/hub outer bearing (later type)

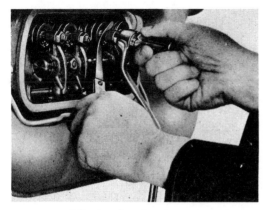

Adjusting the valve clearances

and bend the locktab on early models or tighten the hexagon bolt on later models.

Finally refit the hub cap and wheel cap and lower the car.

15 Check and adjust steering mechanism

Jack up the front of the car and grip each wheel in turn on its side. Try to turn the wheel in alternate directions quite firmly to determine if there's any wear in the steering linkages, steering box, or rack. If you notice any movement, the wear can either be in the linkage or the steering gear. On early models the king pins or balljoints were provided with grease nipples, and in this case it may be possible to eliminate some free play by using a grease gun. If the later type of joint is worn it must be renewed. It's worthwhile checking the condition of the balljoints even if they're not worn, especially the condition of the rubber covers which should be renewed if damaged.

If the steering gear requires adjustment and your car's fitted with a steering box, first check whether the spindle entering the box can be moved up and down. If there's any movement on early models loosen the pinchbolt located on the top of the casing and turn the adjustable sleeve until the movement is eliminated. On later models loosen the large nut on the bottom of the casing and turn the plug. Turn the steering wheel from side to side after the adjustment to make sure you've not overtightened it, and don't forget to tighten the locknut afterwards.

Should there still be play in the steering box you can make a further adjustment which controls the roller to spindle (later models) or sector to worm (early models) clearance. To get at this adjustment you'll have to remove a small metal panel from the back of the spare wheel well. Jack up the front of the car until the wheels are off the ground then turn the steering to the straight ahead position. On early models without the plastic filler plugs, loosen the locknut and turn the adjuster fully in, then back it off $\frac{1}{8}$th of a turn. Tighten the locknut and check that the steering doesn't bind when turned from side to side. On later models with the plastic filler plugs, turn the steering wheel 90° to the left, loosen the locknut, and screw in the adjusting screw until the roller just touches the worm. Turn the steering wheel 90° to the right and check the position required for the screw on this side, then finally set the screw between both settings. Tighten the locknut and lower the car to the ground.

If your car's fitted with rack and pinion type steering, remove the spare wheel and locate the access hole in the luggage compartment floor. Turn the steering straight ahead and loosen the locknut. Unscrew the adjusting screw then screw it in by hand **63**

Rear wheel adjustment and inspection plugs

Checking front wheel bearing free play

Steering box cover location

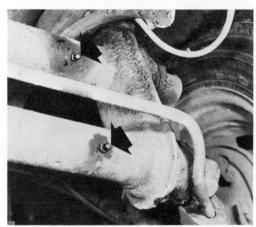

Front axle tube bearing grease points (arrowed)

Removing a windscreen wiper arm

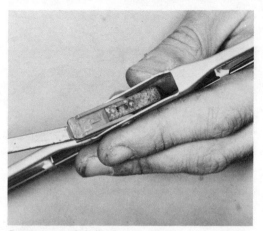

Removing a windscreen wiper blade

only until it just touches the thrust washer. Tighten the locknut while holding the adjusting screw still with a spanner.

Make a final check of the adjustment by driving the car to see if the steering operates smoothly in both directions.

16 Check suspension and lubricate

Jack up the front and rear of the car and generally clean the areas around the springs or torsion bars, shock absorbers and suspension pivots, using a wire brush. In particular check the shock absorbers for leakage and any rubber bushes for wear and deterioration. Any problem areas should be attended to as soon as possible.

On models with torsion bar front suspension a grease gun should be used to lubricate the axle tube bearings; there are two nipples on either side. At the same time it pays to grease the handbrake cable and pedal shaft.

With all four wheels back on the ground, bounce the car on each corner to check the efficiency of the shock absorbers. After releasing the car the bottom of a bounce it should rise one stroke and settle approximately half way down the next. If not, the shock absorber needs renewing.

17 Lubricate generally

Using an oil can filled with engine oil, lubricate the moving parts of the carburettor, handbrake and clutch cables, petrol reserve lever, heater controls, door hinges and locks, engine lid and luggage compartment lid hinges and locks, then lightly grease the door striker plates.

Wipe off any surplus oil or grease before someone else does on their clothing!

18 Check windscreen wiper blades and lubricate spindles

Examine the windscreen wiper blades for wear and renew them if they don't clean the windscreen effectively. During the production run of the Beetle a number of different arrangements for attaching the wiper blades have been introduced, but they're all quite simple and no trouble should be experienced removing the blades. The early types are held in position with a rubber plug; later ones simply clip onto the wiper arms. On some late models the rubber inserts can be renewed by removing a small clip in the blade with a pair of pliers.

After checking the wiper blades, lubricate the spindles and rubber bushes with 1 or 2 drops of glycerine.

19 Clean automatic transmission control valve filter

This is a mushroom shaped unit fitted to the side of the control valve. Unscrew the filter with a spanner on the hexagon shank of the mounting stud, then thoroughly clean it in petrol and shake it dry before refitting it.

EVERY 6000 MILES (10 000 KM) OR 6 MONTHS, WHICHEVER COMES FIRST
(In addition to the checks detailed in the 3000 mile Schedule)

The following tools, lubricants, etc, are likely to be needed:

Valve cover gaskets, feeler gauges, screwdriver, assorted metric spanners, tachometer, distilled water, relined brake shoes, hexagon key, pliers, 36 mm socket.

1 Check valve clearances

This is one of the more critical checks to be made on your Beetle engine, because an incorrectly adjusted valve clearance may not only result in poor engine performance, it could lead to a complete engine overhaul. The adjustment of number 3 cylinder is most important as this cylinder tends to get slightly less cooling from air because the oil cooler is positioned right next to it; a tight clearance could lead to a burnt out valve in quite a short time. With the engine running on three cylinders, the oil overheats and loses its properties with the result that wear rapidly takes place in the main bearings, pistons and cylinders.

The valve clearances must be adjusted with the engine stone cold; it's therefore a good idea to carry out this work after the car has been left stationary overnight.

The first thing to do is to remove the distributor cap and rotate the engine until the rotor is pointing to the line on the distributor body, indicating that number 1 cylinder is in the firing position with the piston at the top of its compression stroke. On the VW engine both valve clearances are adjusted with the relevant cylinder in the firing position and the piston at the top of its stroke, so the timing marks on the crankshaft pulley should now be in line with the crankcase centre line. Check that the handbrake's firmly applied and the gear lever's in neutral. Now lie down on the right-hand side of the car and reach up to the valve cover; if there's any sign of oil leakage you'll have to fit a new gasket after making the adjustment. Prise back the retaining spring then pull the cover away, at the same time catching any oil which may drip.

Number 1 cylinder is the front one on this side so **65**

the two front valve clearances can now be adjusted. First loosen the locknut on each rocker arm adjusting screw, then put a feeler blade of the correct size (see *Vital Statistics*) between the adjuster and the end of the valve stem. Turn the adjusting screw until the feeler blade is a firm sliding fit. Tighten the locknut and check the adjustment again; when you've adjusted one valve check the remaining one on number 1 cylinder.

With number 1 cylinder clearances adjusted turn the engine anticlockwise 180° and check that the distributor rotor has turned anticlockwise by 90°. The valve clearances of number 2 cylinder (rear, right) can now be adjusted in the same manner, after which the valve cover can be refitted together with a new gasket.

The valve clearances for numbers 3 and 4 cylinders are checked in exactly the same way after turning the engine anticlockwise 180° before each check.

2   Adjust carburettor

First run the engine until it reaches its normal operating temperature; a round trip of three or four miles should be sufficient.

If your engine's one of the manual choke type or early automatic choke type without an idle mixture control screw next to the volume control screw, adjust the throttle stop screw so that the engine speed is 700 to 800 rpm. This is a fast tickover and ideally you'll need a tachometer to get the speed just right. Turn the volume control screw clockwise until the speed decreases, then anticlockwise until the engine runs smoothly and evenly. Turn it anticlockwise a further $\frac{1}{4}$ turn, then adjust the throttle stop screw if necessary to achieve the correct idling speed.

If your carburettor's the later type, the most accurate method of adjustment is with a CO (Carbon Monoxide) meter in which case your local VW garage is the best bet. However you can make the following check. With the engine at normal temperature check that the throttle stop screw is resting on the lowest section of the fast idle cam. This indicates that the automatic choke is not in operation. Now using a tachometer check that the engine speed is between 750 and 900 rpm (manual gearbox) or 850 and 1000 rpm (automatic transmission). If not, adjust the bypass idle screw, that's the larger recessed screw, until the speed is correct. The throttle stop screw should not be adjusted, as it's set by the manufacturers and should have a tamperproof plastic tip on it. If a CO meter is not available, turn the mixture screw, that's the small recessed screw, to give the highest engine speed then re-adjust the bypass idle screw to give the correct idling speed.

Distributor rotor position for adjusting valve clearances on cylinders (numbered)

Later bypass idle carburettor adjusting points

1 Throttle stop screw   3 Volume control screw
2 Mixture screw

Carburettor location

3 Clean and check battery

First remove the rear seat cushion. If you've got a hydrometer, now's the time to use it to check your battery specific gravity (SG for short). Assuming that it's fully charged, the SG should be as given in the table according to the battery temperature. If the battery's been on charge recently leave it for an hour or two if you can, as it warms up when being charged.

Electrolyte temperature	SG (fully charged)
100°F or 38°C	1.268
90°F or 32°C	1.272
80°F or 27°C	1.276
70°F or 21°C	1.280
60°F or 16°C	1.284
50°F or 10°C	1.288
40°F or 4°C	1.292
30°F or -1.5°C	1.296

If one cell has a low reading it indicates loss of electrolyte (unlikely unless the casing's cracked) or an internal fault. In either case, the end is in sight — prepare to buy a new one before it lets you down.

From time to time corrosion may appear on the battery terminals or on the ends of the main battery leads. Where this has occurred, detach the leads, remove the battery clamping plate and lift out the battery. A solution of warm water and bicarbonate of soda will remove all the corrosion; brush it on to the terminals, making sure that none gets inside. Dip the lead ends straight into the mixture, but too much corrosion will neutralise it so you may need a second mix. Also clean round the battery compartment if corrosion's visible there too. During all this, take care that the mixture doesn't get into your eyes, as there's a certain amount of splashing and bubbling as it does its work.

When everything's clean again, wipe every part dry with a dry cloth. An underseal type of paint can be used in the battery compartment if there's been corrosion, as this provides a good degree of protection. Other parts should be smeared with petroleum jelly before being bolted up. Make sure that everything's covered, but only very lightly. Refit the battery and leads, (fit the negative lead first) smearing a little petroleum jelly on the lead ends and terminals, then refit the seat cushion.

4 Change round wheels

This can be combined with the next check and should be made in accordance with the accompanying illustration. Note that the direction of wheel rotation stays unchanged with the wheels remaining on the same sides.

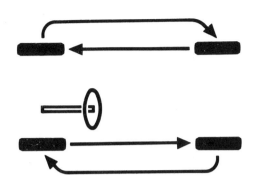

Wheel changing sequence

After changing the wheels always check and adjust the tyre pressures to the new levels.

5 Check brake linings for wear

Front drum brakes

Jack up the front of the car and support it on axle stands. Prise the rubber plugs from the backplates and, with the aid of a torch if necessary, determine the amount of lining remaining on the shoes. If this is less than 2.5 mm, the lining surface is less than 0.5 mm above the rivet heads and the linings must be renewed.

First remove the wheels and the hub cover, noting that a split pin or circlip must be removed from the left-hand side cover first. On early models unscrew the locknut and adjusting nut and on later models loosen the hexagon socket and remove the clamp nut. Remember that the left-hand side nuts have left-hand threads. Lift the drum complete with outer bearing and thrust washer off the stub axle. If this proves difficult it may be necessary to back off the brake adjusters (see 3000 mile Schedule).

Using pliers depress the steady spring retainers, turn them through 90° and remove them with the springs. Note the position of the shoes and retaining springs then unhook the lower or front springs and disengage both shoes from the backplate.

Clean the backplate and brake drum, and if the wheel cylinder shows any signs of leakage, repair or renew it. Check the adjusters for freedom of movement and lubricate them with a little high melting point grease. They must be screwed right in before new brake shoes are fitted.

Fit the new shoes to the backplate using a reversal of the removal procedure, making sure that **67**

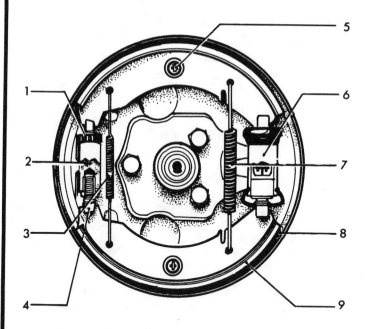

Front brake assembly

1 Adjusting wheel
2 Anchor piece
3 Front retractor spring
4 Adjusting screw
5 Steady pin spring and cup retainer
6 Hydraulic cylinder
7 Rear retractor spring
8 Backplate
9 Brake shoe and lining

Rear brake assembly (manual adjustment)

1 Hydraulic cylinder
2 Brake shoe and lining
3 Upper retractor spring
4 Steady pin, spring and cup retainer
5 Lower retractor spring
6 Adjusting screw
7 Backplate
8 Connecting plate
9 Handbrake connecting lever
10 Handbrake cable
11 Adjusting wheel
12 Anchor piece

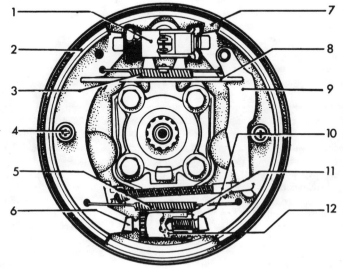

the springs are located correctly and the shoes engage the wheel cylinder and adjuster slots.

Centralise the shoes on the backplate then refit the brake drum. Adjust the wheel bearing and brakes as described in the 3000 mile Schedule.

Rear drum brakes

To check the lining thickness, jack up the rear of the car and support it on axle stands. Prise the rubber plugs from the backplates and check the lining thickness. If the thickness is less than 2.5 mm the shoes must be renewed as follows.

Before jacking up the rear wheels the slotted nuts must be loosened at the end of each axle. To do this you'll need a 36 mm socket and a handle at least one metre long. First remove the wheel cap and the split pin from the castellated nut. Firmly apply the handbrake and loosen the nut, then do the same on the other side. Jack up the rear of the car and support it with axle stands, but leave the wheels secured to the drums. Remove the axle nuts then grip the wheels in turn and ease each drum off the axle shafts. If this method fails to release the drums you'll have to get a special puller from a tool agent.

After removing the drums, note the position of the shoes and retaining springs; then, using pliers, depress the steady spring retainers, turn them through 90° and remove them with the springs.

If you've got manually adjusted rear brake shoes, there's two holes in the backplate adjacent to the adjusters, and with this type first unhook the lower retaining spring and disconnect the handbrake cable. Detach the shoes from the wheel cylinder and remove them with the handbrake lever and strut.

If you've got self-adjusting rear brake shoes the procedure is very similar but you'll have to make a special note of the spring and adjustable strut locations.

Clean the backplate and drum, and check the wheel cylinder for leakage. Lubricate the adjusters (manual adjustment) or adjustable strut (self-adjustment) with high melting point grease and screw the adjustment fully back before fitting new shoes.

The new shoes are fitted using a reversal of the removal procedure making sure that everything's correctly located. Centralise the shoes on the backplate, and on self-adjusting brakes adjust the adjustable strut so that the drum will just go on. Refit the drum and tighten the axle nut moderately, so that the brake shoes can be adjusted as described in the 3000 mile Schedule. On self-adjusting brakes, operate the brake pedal several times until the free play is minimum.

Finally tighten the axle nut to 253 lbf ft (35 kgf m) and insert the split pin.

6 Check wheel alignment and balance

This check is best entrusted to a suitably equipped garage, although there are a number of fairly accurate devices on sale in some accessory shops. If you've got one of these, follow the manufacturer's instructions; we've listed the correct alignment details in *Vital Statistics.*

7 Check brake and fuel pipes

These should be thoroughly checked for leaks, chafing, corrosion, and general deterioration. Any suspect pipes must be renewed; seek advice from your local VW garage.

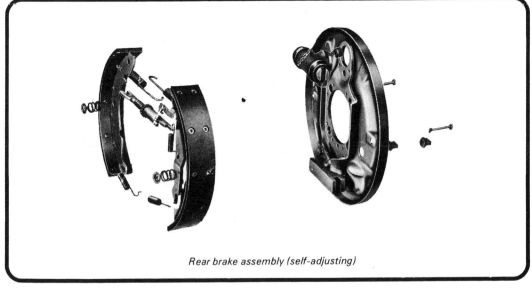

Rear brake assembly (self-adjusting)

8 Check steering box oil level

On models fitted with the early type steering box, remove the metal panel in the luggage compartment, unscrew the filler plug, and top up the oil level as necessary. Later models fitted with two plastic plugs are filled with grease and should not require topping up.

9 Check driveshafts

On early models examine the flexible gaiters at the transmission end of the axle tubes. On later models fitted with double jointed driveshafts, check the shafts for wear and the flexible gaiters for damage. Where necessary arrange with your local VW garage to have repairs undertaken.

10 Other checks

Check the engine and transmission mountings for deterioration and security, then generally check the security of all accessible components on the car, in particular the following items; starter motor, front and rear suspension mountings, steering column clamp, steering gear mounting, carburettor and manifold mounting nuts, and exhaust mountings.

EVERY 12 000 MILES (20 000 KM) OR 12 MONTHS, WHICHEVER COMES FIRST
(In addition to the checks detailed in the 6000 mile Schedule)
The following tools, lubricants, etc are likely to be needed:

New spark plugs, new air cleaner element (where applicable), contact breaker points.

1 Fit new spark plugs

All the information for this job will be found in the 3000 mile Service Schedule. Make sure that the new plugs are the correct type for your particular model.

2 Fit new air cleaner element

This only applies to later models and all the information necessary for this job will be found in the 3000 mile Service Schedule.

3 Fit new distributor contact breaker points

All the information for this job will be found in the 3000 mile Service Schedule. Recheck the ignition timing after fitting.

EVERY 24 000 MILES (40 000 KM) OR 2 YEARS, WHICHEVER COMES FIRST
(In addition to the checks detailed in the 12 000 mile Schedule)
The following tools, lubricants etc are likely to be needed:

Front hub bearing grease, paraffin.

Repack front hub bearings with grease

The information for the removal of the front drums is given in the 6000 mile Service Schedule, and the front brake shoes should also be removed. If your car's got front disc brakes, remove the caliper and suspend it with a piece of wire, then remove the hub using the same procedure as with the drum.

Using a brush and paraffin, clean all of the grease from the bearings and hub then dry all the components, preferably with an air line. Coat the bearings and the space between them in the hub with liberal quantities of lithium based grease. Refit all the components in the reverse order of removal and adjust the bearings as described in the 3000 mile Schedule. You should not, however, put any grease in the hub caps.

EVERY 30 000 MILES (50 000 KM) OR 30 MONTHS, WHICHEVER COMES FIRST
The following tools, lubricants, etc, are likely to be needed:

Gearbox oil, hexagon drain plug key, or metric socket (automatic transmission models).

Change automatic transmission gearbox oil

The oil should be changed when warm. To do this place a container of at least 3.5 litres (6.2 pints) capacity beneath the transmission and remove the drain and filler plugs. On some models you'll have to remove the pan from the bottom of the gearbox as no drain plug is provided; there are 14 screws altogether.

Automatic transmission filler and level plug (A) and drain plug (B)

After all the oil has drained out, clean the magnetic plugs or the pan and refit them. Where the complete pan is removed, renew the gasket if it's unserviceable and tighten the screws in diagonal sequence to 7 lbf ft (1 kgf m).

Refill the gearbox slowly with the correct grade oil and check that the level is to the bottom of the filler hole. Finally tighten the filler plug into the casing.

EVERY 36 000 MILES (60 000 KM) OR 3 YEARS, WHICHEVER COMES FIRST

Discuss with your local VW garage the advisability of having new hydraulic brake seals, hoses and fluid fitted. Much will depend on how much moisture has been accumulated by the hydraulic fluid, and some garages are equipped to make an accurate check of this. If the work is necessary, it's best entrusted to a VW garage who will have the necessary facilities for doing it.

OTHER REGULAR MAINTENANCE

If you carry out the procedures we've detailed so far, at more or less the prescribed intervals of mileage or time, then you'll have gone a long way towards getting the best out of your Beetle in terms of both performance and long life.

That's the good news. The other kind is that there are always other areas not dealt with in regular servicing schedules, where neglect can spell trouble.

We reckon a bit of extra time spent on your car at the beginning and end of the winter will be repaid in terms of peace of mind and prevention of trouble. The suggested attentions which follow have been divided into Spring and Autumn sections — but there's nothing to prevent you doing them more frequently if you like.

SPRING

We've put this one first as it's less depressing than Autumn — though there's probably more work involved.

Underside of car

In Spring, we venture to suggest, the owner's fancy turns to thoughts of cleaning of all the accumulated muck of winter from underneath the car. Without a shadow of doubt, the best time to clean underneath is the worst time from the discomfort point of view — that is, when the car's been driven in the wet and all the dirt's nicely softened up. So let's talk first about the easier way out — steam cleaning or pressure washing. These are not D-I-Y jobs, and can

only be done at larger garages, usually those which undertake body repair jobs. You may feel that this method's unnecessarily expensive, but it's generally preferable to grovelling about underneath and getting filthy and uncomfortable doing it yourself. However, for the owner who really wants to do it by hand, here goes ...

You'll need paraffin or a water soluble solvent, water (and preferably a hose), a wire brush, a scraper and a stiff-bristle brush. If you think the car floor may leak, remove the carpets or they'll get wet; this will also help you pinpoint the places where the water's getting in.

To start with, jack the car up as high as possible, preferably at one side or one end. For your own safety, support it on ramps or concrete or wooden blocks and chock the wheels which are on the ground. Unless both rear wheels are raised, also apply the handbrake, and engage first or reverse gear.

Now get underneath (you've put it off as long as you can!) and cover the brake discs and calipers with polythene bags to stop mud and water getting into them. Next loosen any encrusted dirt and, working from one end or one side, scrape or brush this away. The paraffin or solvent can be used where there's oil contamination. After all the brushing and scraping, a final wash down with the hose will remove the last of the dirt and mud.

You can now check for leaks in the floor. If you find any, dry the area carefully then use a mastic type sealer to plug the offending gap. Hollow sections of doors and bodywork can be sprayed or brush-painted with a rust inhibitor to provide some extra protection. If there are signs of the underseal breaking away, this is a good opportunity to patch it up. Undersealing paint's available in spray cans or tins from accessory shops; one small point about putting the stuff on though, and that's to make sure the area is clean and dry, otherwise you're wasting your time.

While you're underneath, have a good look round for signs of rusting. Likely places are side runners, floor panels and chassis sections. If you find any, have a word with your VW man or body repair shop before things get too bad.

Bodywork

This too will have suffered from all the muck and salt that's around during the winter, and there's no better time than now to wash it thoroughly and check for stone chips and rust spots. You're bound to find some, despite the regular washing you've given the car — or meant to — throughout the winter. Treat as for rusty scratches (see *Body Beautiful*).

After the touch up paint's thoroughly hardened, it's worth giving the car a good polish to prepare it for the long, hot summer ahead (well, there's no harm in **71**

Ignition leads and distributor cap – items for spray on water dispersant

hoping). If you're feeling really energetic you could do the interior as well (*Body Beautiful* again) but the most important cleaning jobs are done now.

AUTUMN

With winter on the way your car's electrical system is going to take much more of a beating than it has during the last few months. Now – and not on a dark night miles from anywhere in a snowstorm – is the time to check the vital components. Where other Sections or Chapters are referred to in brackets, the detailed procedure's described there.

Battery

Ensure that this is topped up correctly (*Weekly Section*).

Fan belt

Check and adjust or renew as necessary (*3000 miles*).

Lights

Check operation (*Weekly Section*).

Renew any failed bulbs (*In an Emergency*) or check for faults as necessary (*Troubleshooter 6*).

Wipers/Washers

These are going to get a lot of use so check the wiper arms and blades (*3000 miles*).

Top up washer reservoir (*Weekly Section*) and check operation.

Tyres

Check tread and condition (*Weekly Section*). Remember that you may well be driving in slippery conditions.

Bodywork

Finally, if you've got any energy left, wash the car and polish it thoroughly to help protect the paint against the winter elements.

Aerosol products

In damp and foggy weather some parts of the electrical system tend to get covered in moisture and the answer for this problem is to use one of the proprietary spray-on water dispersants.

Body Beautiful

If you've bought this book intending to do all the routine servicing of your car yourself, then you'll surely want to keep the bodywork and inside of the car looking good too. And for anyone who doesn't here's how to do it anyway ...

It's always a good idea to clean the interior first; this way you won't get the dust all over your nicely polished exterior – or the car's! Begin by removing all the contents, not forgetting the odds and ends in the pockets and glovebox. Then take out all the mats and carpets, which should be shaken and brushed, or better still vacuum-cleaned. If they need further cleaning this can be done with a carpet shampoo, but let them dry thoroughly before you put them back. Any underfelt should be taken out and shaken, too, but don't try washing this or it may end up in rather more pieces than you started with.

If the carpets should just happen to be in such a bad state of decay that they don't merit cleaning, why not get yourself a decent set of replacements? You can get kits tailored for your particular model from specialist firms, and they're quite reasonably priced.

The inside of the car can now be cleaned with a brush and dustpan, or again preferably a vacuum-cleaner. If the flex on the Hoover won't stretch to the car (and the car won't squeeze through the front door!) it might be worth thinking about investing in one of the small 12 volt hand vacuums which can be attached to your car battery – your accessory shop can probably show you one.

Seat and trim materials can be wiped over with warm water containing a little washing-up liquid, but for best results (particularly if they're very dirty) use one of the proprietary upholstery cleaners which are specially made for the job. An old nail brush will help to remove ingrained marks, but don't splash too much water about and do wipe the surfaces dry afterwards with a clean cloth, leaving the windows open to speed up drying. The carpets can be put back when they're quite dry, making sure they're properly fitted around the controls etc.

You have to be careful about cleaning car windows, especially the windscreen, with some household products as these can leave a smeary film. Water containing a few drops of ammonia is probably best, but any stubborn marks and smears can be removed with methylated spirit; finish off with a chamois leather squeezed as dry as possible.

Just in case you should think that's it, there's still the front luggage compartment to be dealt with. Take out that collection of junk that seems to have grown every time you open the lid, and get busy with brush or vacuum cleaner again. While you're at it, if you must carry all that stuff around, now's the time to try and stow it so it doesn't rattle any more!

Now you can pause for a moment – make a well earned cup of tea perhaps – and take a critical look at the interior. Are there any nicks or tears in the seats or other trim? Is the headlining drooping or peeling? Some excellent products can now be obtained for repairs such as these. One of the most useful is probably the vinyl repair kit, which comes in various colours and consists of a quantity of 'liquid vinyl' and some sheets of texturing material. The liquid is applied to a split or hole in a plastic seat or piece of trim, smoothed like body filler, and allowed to set. It's then blended into the surrounding area by selecting the best matching pattern from the graining material supplied, placing this over the repair and rubbing with a hot iron; the pattern is then embossed in the repaired area. This type of repair's equally successful, incidentally, on vinyl roofs if your car happens to have one.

For larger splits or tears it may be necessary to cut a piece of matching material from somewhere that doesn't show, apply some suitable adhesive to it and work it under the edges of the tear, pressing these together as neatly as possible once the glue has become tacky enough. Any loose headlining or trim 73

Likely rusting points on the VW Beetle models

can also be stuck in place — but make sure you get an adhesive that's suitable for PVC or vinyl.

Once you've got the seats in a reasonable state of cleanliness and repair, why not consider seat covers? Like the carpets, they're available from specialist firms to suit your car and are a worthwhile buy in view of the protection they give.

If you use your car regularly and you've got the time and inclination, it should really be washed every week, either by hand (preferably using a hosepipe) or by taking advantage of the local car-wash if there is one. Whichever method you choose (assuming you wash your car at all!) we don't think we need tell you how to do it — but remember it's never a good idea to just wipe over a very dirty car, whether wet or dry; you might as well sandpaper it!

Two or three times a year (even once is better than not at all) a good silicone or wax polish can be used on the paintwork. We don't know which of the many makes you'll use, so we can only recommend you to follow the maker's instructions closely so that you do see a reward for your efforts. Chrome parts are best cleaned with a special chrome cleaner; ordinary metal polish will attack the finish.

If the paint's beginning to lose its gloss or colour, and ordinary polishing doesn't seem to help, it will be worth considering the use of a polish with a mild 'cutting' action to remove what is, in effect, a surface layer of dead paint. Your friendly neighbourhood accessory shop man will advise on a suitable type.

The remainder of this Chapter describes how to keep your car's bodywork and paintwork in good condition by dealing with scratches and more major damage too, as they occur. A number of repair aids and materials are referred to, most of them essential if you're to achieve good results. They should all be available, together with free advice, from good motor accessory shops.

Keeping paintwork up to scratch

With superficial scratches (the sort only other people seem to get) where they don't penetrate down to the metal, you'll be glad to hear that repair can be very simple. Lightly rub the area with a paintwork renovator or a fine cutting paste to remove any loose paint from the scratch and to clean off any polish. Rinse the area with plenty of clean water and allow to dry. Apply touch-up paint to the scratch using a fine brush, and continue to build up the paint by several applications, allowing each to dry, until it's level with the surrounding area. Allow the new paint at least two weeks to harden (knitting or a crossword puzzle will help to pass the time), then use the paintwork renovator or cutting paste again to blend it into the original. Now a good polish can be used.

When you've got a scratch that's penetrated right through to the metal, causing rusting, you need a different technique. Use your Scout knife to remove any loose rust from the bottom of the scratch, then paint on a rust-inhibiting paint to prevent it from spreading. You'll probably now need to apply cellulose body stopper paste — use a rubber or nylon applicator or a knife, but don't borrow one from the kitchen as you'll have a job cleaning it!

The paste can be thinned down if necessary using cellulose thinners. Before it hardens, it's a good idea to wrap a piece of smooth cotton rag round the end of your finger, dip it in thinners and quickly sweep it across the filled scratch. This ensures that the area is very slightly hollowed and allows the paint to be built up to the correct level as described earlier.

Dealing with dents

When your car's bodywork gets a deep depression, you'll probably have one too. But there's no reason why even fairly large dents can't be tackled successfully by the D-I-Y owner, especially using the excellent body repair materials now available. So cheer up, and let's see what can be done.

The first step is to try to pull the dented metal out to bring it more or less back to the original level. Don't expect to make a perfect job of this — you won't; the metal has stretched and 'work-hardened' which makes it a virtually impossible job. Try to bring the level up to about $\frac{1}{8}$ inch below the surrounding area; obviously, with shallow dents you can bypass this bit. If the underside of the dent can be got at, try hammering it out gently from behind using a hammer with a wooden or plastic head. You'll need to hold a fairly heavy hardwood block on the outside of the dent; this absorbs the impact of the hammer blows and helps to stop the metal being dented in the opposite direction!

If you've got a dent in a completely enclosed body section, or there's something else preventing you from getting behind it, a different approach is needed. Try to screw up enough courage to drill several small holes through the metal in the dent, particularly in the deeper parts. Now screw in several self-tapping screws so that they get a good bite, and either pull on the heads with pliers or wrap some heavy gauge steel wire round them and pull this. Brace yourself in case something gives suddenly or you may dent your own bodywork!

Now to remove the paint from the damaged area. This is best done using a power drill and abrasive disc, but if you've got the time and energy you can use elbow-grease and abrasive paper. Don't forget to remove the paint from an inch or so of the surrounding good paintwork, too, so that everything blends in nicely. Now score the metal surface with a **75**

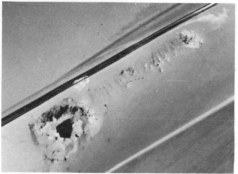

The procedure given with these photos is simplified; more comprehensive instructions will be found in the accompanying text. Typical rust damage is shown here, but the procedure for the repair of dents and gashes is similar.

First remove fittings from the immediate area and then remove loose rust and paint. A wire brush or abrasive disc mounted in a power drill is best, although the job can be done by hand. You need to be very thorough.

The edges of a hole should be tapped inwards with a hammer to provide a hollow for the filler. Having done this, apply rust inhibitor to the affected area (including the underside where possible) and allow this to dry thoroughly.

Before attempting to fill larger holes, block them off with suitable material. Metal tape can be used, but the picture shows a piece of aluminium gauze being sized up for use on this hole.

When mixing the body filler, follow the manufacturers' instructions very carefully. Mix thoroughly, don't mix too much at one go, and don't make it up until you're ready to start filling - modern fillers begin to harden very quickly!

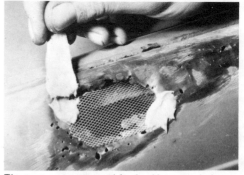

The tape or gauze used for backing up a hole can be secured in position with a few small blobs of filler paste. It's a good idea to mix a very small quantity for this purpose first.

After mixing the filler, apply it quickly with a flexible applicator, following the contours of the body. The filler should be built up in successive thin layers, the final one being just above the level of the surrounding bodywork.

A fairly coarse file or cutting tool is best for removing excess filler and for achieving the initial contour. Care must be taken not to overdo the filing or you'll hollow out the surface and have to fill it again!

A sanding block will now be needed; this can be made of wood as shown or a purpose-made rubber one can be purchased. Begin shaping the filler by using the block with progressively finer grades of dry abrasive paper, followed by ...

... wet and-dry paper, keeping both the work area and the paper wet. Rubbing down is complete when the filled area is 'feathered' into the surrounding painted areas, as shown; this final stage is achieved with the finest grade paper.

After thorough washing and drying, any necessary masking can be done and a coat of primer applied. Again, build this up with successive thin layers. Once the primer is dry it should be smoothed with very fine wet-and-dry paper.

The top coat of paint can now be applied, again in thin layers. Later a mild cutting paste can be used to blend it with the surrounding paint. Finish off with a good quality polish.

screwdriver or the tang of a file to provide a good key for the filler which you're going to have to apply, in case you didn't know. Now, to finish off the repair, refer to the filling and spraying section at the end of this Chapter.

Rust holes and gashes

If there's any paint left on the affected area, remove it as described above so that you can get a good idea of just how bad the problem is. If there's more rust or fresh air than good metal, now's the time to consider whether a replacement panel would be more appropriate; this is a body shop job beyond the scope of this book.

If things don't seem that bad and you're prepared to have a go at doing the job yourself, remove all the fittings from the surrounding area except those which may help to give a good guide to what the shape should be (eg headlamp shells). Now, get a hacksaw blade or a pair of snips and cut out all the loose and badly affected metal. Hammer the edges inwards so that you've got a recessed area to build up on.

Wire brush the edges to remove any powdery rust, then paint over with a rust inhibitor; if you can get to the back, do the same to that. You're now going to fill the hole with something, but unfortunately just anything won't do. The best bets are zinc gauze, aluminium tape or polyurethane foam. The gauze is probably the favourite for a large hole. Cut a piece slightly larger than the hole to be filled, then position it in the hole so that its edges are below the level of the surrounding bodywork. If necessary, hold it in place with a few blobs of filler paste. For small or narrow holes you can use the aluminium tape which is sold by the roll. Pull off a piece and trim to the approximate size and shape required. If there's backing paper, peel it off (it sticks better that way) and place the tape over the hole; if necessary, pieces can be overlapped at the edges. Burnish down the edges of the tape with a file handle or similar to make sure it's firmly adhering to the metal.

Polyurethane foam is best used in hollow body sections but, if you're using this, follow the maker's instructions carefully. When this foam hardens it can be cut back to just below the level of the surrounding bodywork with a hacksaw blade.

With the hole now blocked off, the affected area can be filled and sprayed as follows.

Filling and spraying

Many types of body filler are available, but generally speaking those proprietary kits which contain filler paste (or filler powder and resin liquid) and a separate hardener are best. You'll also need a flexible plastic or nylon applicator (usually supplied) for putting the mixture on with. Mix up a little of the filler on a piece of board or plastic (those plastic margarine tubs are ideal but do wash out all traces of the contents first!). Read the instructions carefully and don't make up too much at one go. You'll find you have to work fairly fast or the mixture will begin to set, especially if you've been a bit generous with the hardener.

Apply the paste to the prepared hole or dent more or less to the correct level and contour, but don't try to shape it once it's become tacky or it'll pick up on the applicator. Layers should be built up at intervals until the final level's just proud of the surrounding bodywork.

When the filler has fully hardened, use a Surform plane or coarse file to remove the excess and obtain the final shape. Then follow with progressively finer grades of wet-or-dry abrasive paper starting with coarse, followed by medium, then fine (some manufacturers give 'grit' grades to their wet-or-dry paper – 40 is the coarsest, 400 the finest). Always wrap the paper round a flat block if you're trying to get a flat surface, and keep it wet by rinsing in clean water or the filler and paint will clog up the abrasive surface.

At this point, the doctored area should be surrounded by a ring of bare metal, encircled by a feathered edge of good paintwork. Rinse it with plenty of clean water to get rid of all the paint and filler dust, and allow it to dry completely.

If you're happy with the surface you've obtained, then you're ready to apply some paint. First spray over the whole area with a light coat of grey primer. This will show up any surface imperfections which may need further treatment, and will also help you get the knack of spraying with an aerosol can before you start on the colour coats. Rub down the surface again, and if necessary use a little body stopper, as described for minor scratches, to fill any small imperfections. Repeat this spray-and-level procedure until you're satisfied with the finish; then wash down again and allow to dry.

The next stage is to apply the finishing coats, but first a word or two about the techniques involved. Paint spraying should be done in a warm, dry, windless, dust-free atmosphere – conditions not very readily available to most of us! You may be able to approach them artificially if you've got a large indoor workshop, but if you have to work outside you'll need to pick the day carefully. If you're working in your garage you'll probably need to 'lay' the dust on the floor by damping it with water.

If the body repair's confined to a small patch, mask off the surrounding area to protect it from paint spray. Bodywork fitting (chrome strips, door handles and the like) will need to be either masked or removed. If you're masking, use genuine masking tape and plenty of newspaper as necessary. Before starting to spray, shake the aerosol can thoroughly; then experiment on something (an old tin or similar will do — not the neighbours' car!) until you feel you can apply the paint smoothly. At the previous stage this wasn't too important, but now you're trying to get the best possible finish.

First cover the repair area with a thick coat of primer — not as one coat, but built up of several thin ones. When this is dry, using the finest wet-or-dry paper, rub down the surface until it's really smooth. Use plenty of water to keep the surface clean; when it's dry, spray on another primer coat and repeat the procedure.

Now for the top coat. Again the idea's to build up the paint thickness by several thin coats. Have a test spray first as this is a different aerosol, then commence spraying in the centre of the repair area. Using a circular motion, work gradually outwards towards the edges until the whole of the repair and about two inches of the surrounding original paint is covered. Remove all the masking material 10 to 15 minutes after you've finished spraying.

Now you can start putting away all the bits and pieces because it'll need about two weeks for the paint to harden completely. After this time, using a paint renovator or a very fine cutting paste, blend the edges of the new paint into the original. Finally, apply a good wax or silicone polish, and hopefully you'll have a repair you're proud to own up to!

Adding 'pinstripes'

There are various kinds of self-adhesive body decor available for customising your car. Perhaps the neatest and most suitable of the 'add-on' variety are 'pinstripes', and we've mentioned these here as they may appeal to the owner who wants a cheap and simple way to improve the appearance of his or her car. 'Pinstripes' are an adhesive tape which comes in different widths and colours, and as single or multi-stripes. Most have a backing paper which is peeled off as the stripe's applied.

When applying any of these self-adhesive tapes, first make sure the paintwork's clean by washing with warm water and a car shampoo or liquid detergent. Next clean up the surface with a very fine cutting paste or paintwork renovator, and wash down again. You can now apply the tape, but follow the directions carefully. Smooth it down with clean rag and, if necessary, prick out any small air bubbles with a pin. Try not to stretch the stripes as you put them on because they'll shrink slightly anyway; and wrap the ends round the panels so that they don't pull away at the edges.

The Personal Touch

On the subject of accessories it's been said that, if somebody makes it, the motorist will buy it. The 'aftermarket' in extras and accessories has now grown to enormous proportions, and it can be difficult to sort out the useful and practical items from what, at the other end of the scale, is some undoubted rubbish.

We'd need several volumes to discuss all the various kinds of things you might conceivably buy for your car, and those we have managed to mention can't be gone into in great detail in a book like this. Some time spent browsing around a good motor accessory shop will reveal more than we can here, but nevertheless we hope the suggestions given may prove useful.

All good products will be supplied with general fitting instructions which may or may not require minor modifications to suit your Beetle. If you're buying secondhand, of course, you may get no instructions at all. The guidelines given here are in no way intended to replace the manufacturer's instructions, and if you're in doubt about fitting a particular item, they're the people to refer to.

Note: always disconnect the battery before commencing any work involving the electrical system. Fireworks are pretty, but there's a time and place for everything!

Auxiliary instruments

It would be possible to write a complete book just on auxiliary instruments and how to fit them but, as with other things, you'll normally get pretty good instructions when you buy them. Because there are so many instruments available, we're only going to consider those items that are more commonly fitted.

A point to consider before rushing into your nearest accessory shop to buy the latest and greatest in instruments or auto-gadgets, is whether or not it's suitable for your model and also where it can be fitted. The Beetle facia is not over-accommodating in this respect although there is some room in the centre and extreme ends, and some instruments such as tachometers can be of the 'pod' type and will fit on top of the facia.

Sooner or later you're going to have to start drilling some holes somewhere, but this needn't cause any real headaches if it's approached in the right way. Make sure there's nothing behind the panel before even considering drilling a hole, and that there's enough room to fit the instrument, switch, or whatever, in the space chosen. Any hole which will have a cable or capillary running through it must have a plastic or rubber grommet to prevent the metal chafing through; these grommets can be obtained from DIY accessory or car electrical shops.

When it comes to drilling larger holes for instruments, start off by centre-punching the middle of the area, then use compasses or dividers to mark the hole, allowing a little for clearance (standard instruments are 2 inch/52 mm diameter). It's best to mark another hole inside the first hole, and drill around this line so that the centre part can readily be pushed out; if you're using a $\frac{1}{8}$ in drill the inner circle will need to be $\frac{1}{16}$ in inside the first circle marked. Finish the job off by carefully filing and deburring the hole.

Ammeter

The ammeter must be connected in such a way that it registers all the current drawn from or supplied to the battery with the exception of the starting circuit. The wire size for connecting the ammeter should be at least 84/0.30.

If your car's got a 6 volt system, first locate the starter solenoid and find the terminal with the heavy lead which comes from the battery. On the same terminal you'll find one or two smaller leads, and these must be disconnected and joined together if there's two of them. Connect one side of the ammeter to these wires and the other side to the solenoid terminal or the battery terminal which is NOT earthed.

Some of the supplementary instruments and other accessories available from Smiths Industries

If you've got a 12 volt system, locate the battery positive (+) terminal where you'll find two leads, one thick, the other smaller. The smaller one must be disconnected and the ammeter connected between. Remember to solder and insulate all the wiring connections.

If after the connector's connected, it's found to be indicating charge instead of discharge and vice versa, simply reverse the connections at the back of the gauge, but do remember to disconnect the battery earth lead when doing this.

Battery condition indicator

This is simply a voltmeter and must be connected to a good earth point on the chassis and to any suitable connection which is live when the ignition switch is 'on'. For convenience this could be the accessory terminal of the ignition switch or the switch side of an ignition controlled fuse. You won't need heavy cables for the battery condition indicator, 14/0·30 should be OK, but make sure that the polarity's correct.

Clock

Clocks come in many forms, but most types contain semi-conductors. If this means nothing else to you, it means that there's negligible load on the battery and that the polarity's critical if you don't want to cause permanent damage. Connections are much the same as for the battery condition indicator, except that you don't want the clock to stop when the ignition's switched off. Therefore a suitable connecting point should be a fuse which isn't controlled by the ignition switch.

Tachometer

The tachometer (rev counter) is one instrument that's available in larger sizes than the others (80 mm instead of 52 mm, although the smaller sizes can be obtained). Most are positive *or* negative earth, but you must connect them up correctly. If you should pick up a secondhand one, connections for the most common types are shown in the illustrations. Note that with the Smiths type, the distributor-to-coil LT lead is removed; also note the sleeve colours on the main white lead. Use a 14/0·30 (14/0·012) cable size.

Oil pressure gauge

There are two main types of oil pressure gauge, the capillary type and the electrical sender type. For both types you can use the oil pressure switch tapping which is just behind (think about it) number 4 cylinder. If you use a T-piece you can retain the original pressure switch as well. The manufacturer's instructions should clearly explain how to connect up the gauge.

Vacuum gauge (performance gauge or fuel consumption gauge)

This gauge must be connected into the inlet manifold and it informs the driver of the engine operating condition under various work loads. Most types are supplied with a small clamp which is used to restrict the pulsating flow in the flexible pipe to the gauge; it's tightened until the smoothest possible gauge indication is obtained.

Lamps

When auxiliary lamps are fitted, not only must you fit them in a suitable place on the car, but that place must also meet certain legal requirements; where these apply we've attempted to give some guidelines.

In addition to the actual lights themselves, we have to think of the switch (not normally difficult because many small switch panels are available) fusing, cable sizes and whether relays are necessary.

Spot and front fog lamps

It's illegal to mount these with the lower edge of the illuminating surface *more than* 1200 mm (47.24 in) from the ground. Any lamps that are mounted with this lower edge *less than* 500 mm (19.69 in) above the ground may only be used in fog or falling snow. In conditions where the law requires headlamps to be used, eg at night on an unlit road, a single lamp may be used only *in conjunction with* the headlamps. In

these conditions the lamps must always be mounted and used in pairs (two fog, two spot or one of each) if they're to be used independently of the headlamps.

Their outer edges must be *within* 400 mm (15.75 in) of the edge of the car and (in the case of vehicles first used before January 1, 1971 only) their inner edges must be *not less than* 350 mm (13.78 in) apart. If they're used as spotlamps, they should conform to the normal anti-dazzle requirements, eg by wiring them so that they go out when the headlamps are dipped, or by angling them slightly downwards.

Choose the lamps carefully, and if possible match the lamp styles. There are many good types on sale, so if you're not sure what you want ask for advice. The actual mounting is not too difficult; they can either be fitted to a bumper bracket or attached by a separate bracket to the front grille.

To prevent overloading of the existing wiring, a relay should be used (the Lucas 6RA type, part No 33213, is suitable). This is connected through the switch from the existing headlamp circuit to one of the relay 'coil' terminals, the other going to a good earth point. The lamp wires then go to one of the relay 'contact' terminals, with the other terminal being connected either to the battery or the battery connection at the starter solenoid, via a line fuse. The fuse rating will depend on the lamp manufacturers' recommendations, but will probably be about 20 amps for a pair of lamps.

Rear fog lamps

These can often be mounted in much the same way as reversing lamps, although bumper-mounting types are popular; in fact some lamps serve a dual function in having a clear lens for reversing and a red snap-on lens for the warning lamp.

Under the Road Vehicles (Rear Fog Lamps) Regulations 1978, the fitting of at least one rear fog lamp will become compulsory on cars manufactured on or after October 1, 1979 and first used on or after

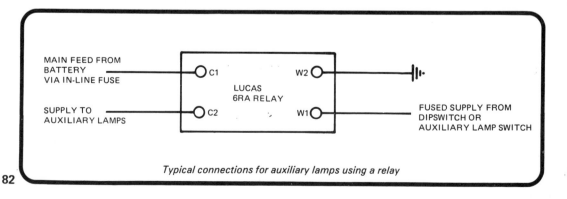

Typical connections for auxiliary lamps using a relay

MAIN FEED FROM BATTERY VIA IN-LINE FUSE — C1

SUPPLY TO AUXILIARY LAMPS — C2

LUCAS 6RA RELAY

W2 —

W1 — FUSED SUPPLY FROM DIPSWITCH OR AUXILIARY LAMP SWITCH

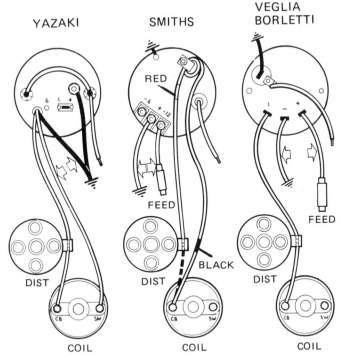

YAZAKI   SMITHS   VEGLIA BORLETTI

Connections for three popular tachometers

Yazaki: *Negative earth shown – reverse arrowed wires to change polarity.*
Smiths: *Positive earth shown – the dotted connection must be removed when the tachometer is fitted. Reverse arrowed wires to change polarity.*
Verglia Borletti: *Negative earth shown – reverse arrowed wires to change polarity.*

April 1, 1980. These same regulations lay down specific rules on the use and positioning of such lamps.

Either one or two lamps may be fitted. If only one is used, it must be on the centre line or to the offside of the car, and *at least* 100 mm (3.94 in) from the nearest brake light. No rear fog lamp is to be illuminated by the braking system of the car. The rear fog lamp switch must have a warning light to indicate to the driver when the lamps are switched on, and this switch must be wired in such a way that the rear fog lamp(s) cannot be used without either headlights, sidelights or front fog lamps also being on.

Any rear fog lamp fitted to a car manufactured from October 1, 1979 must also bear the appropriate 'E-mark' signifying conformity with EEC standards. If your car was manufactured prior to that date (and that includes nearly all the models covered in this Handbook) then you *need* not fit rear fog lamps at all; but if you do (and it obviously makes sense to do so) they must comply with the above regulations con-cerning positioning and independence of the brake lights.

Conditions requiring the use of rear fog lamps obviously also call for headlamps and/or front fog lamps. While front fog lamps may be used only in fog or falling snow, rear fog lamps are to be permitted in conditions of poor visibility when only headlamps may be allowable at the front. It's suggested there-fore, that if you fit rear fog lamps they're wired using a relay, the actuating circuit of which is operated by the sidelight circuit (ie the supply to terminal 'W1' in our relay diagram would come from a sidelight circuit connection).

Anti-theft devices

There are three main categories of car thieves – those people who want your car either as a complete item or for the major mechanical and body parts; those who are out for a joy-ride; and those who merely want the contents. With any type of thief it makes sense to do what you can to prevent someone **83** from wanting to get in; don't leave valuables lying about, don't leave the car unlocked and, if it's parked at home, put it in a locked garage if possible. But if a car thief decides he wants your particular car, statistically he's got a pretty good chance of getting it!

Most models are fitted with a steering column lock which is a very effective protection against a car being driven away, but it still makes sense to have a good burglar alarm fitted. Many types are available, and may be wired into door courtesy light switches or hidden switches beneath the seats. Most types are wired into the car horn circuit but separate horns and bells are available; the more unconventional it is (whilst still being reliable!) the better. Don't put hidden switches in the first place you think of — it might be the first place the thief thinks of too.

Some anti-theft devices are activated by the movement caused through somebody trying to get into the car (and occasionally by an innocent passer-by!). Some not only sound alarms, but also earth the ignition circuit, other devices simply mechanically lock together the steering wheel and brake pedal. Have a look round the accessory shops and see what suits your car, your pocket and the degree of protection required.

Radios and tape players

A radio or tape player is an expensive item to buy, and will only give its best performance if fitted properly. It's useless to expect concert hall performance from a unit that's suspended from the dash panel by string with its speaker resting on the back seat or parcel shelf! If you don't wish to do the installation yourself there are many in-car entertainment specialists who can do the fitting for you.

Make sure the unit purchased is of the same polarity as the car, or that units with adjustable polarity are correctly set before commencing installation.

It's difficult to give specific information with regard to fitting, as final positioning of the radio/tape player, speakers and aerial is entirely a matter of personal preference. However the following paragraphs give guidelines to follow, which are relevant to all installations.

Radios

Most radios are a standardised size of 7 inches wide, by 2 inches deep — this ensures that they'll fit into the radio aperture provided in many cars. The following points should be borne in mind before deciding exactly where to fit the unit:

(a) *The unit must be within easy reach of the driver wearing a seat belt*

(b) *The unit must not be mounted close to an electric tachometer, the ignition switch and its wiring, or the flasher unit and associated wiring*

(c) *The unit must be mounted within reach of the aerial lead, and in such a place that the aerial lead will not have to be routed near the components detailed in paragraph 'b'*

(d) *The unit should not be positioned in a place where it might cause injury to the car occupants in an accident; for instance, under the dash panel above the driver's or passenger's legs*

(e) *The unit must be fitted really securely*

The type of aerial used, and where you're going to fit it, is a matter of personal preference. In general, the taller the aerial, the better reception but there are limits to what is practicable. If you can, fit a fully retractable type — it saves an awful lot of problems with vandals and car-wash equipment. When choosing a suitable spot for the aerial, remember the following points:

(a) *The aerial lead should be as short as possible*

(b) *The aerial should be mounted as far away from the distributor and HT leads as possible*

(c) *The part of the aerial which protrudes beneath the mounting point must not foul the roadwheels, or anything else*

(d) *If possible the aerial should be positioned so that the coaxial lead does not have to be routed through the engine compartment*

(e) *The aerial should be mounted at a more-or-less vertical angle*

Tape players

Fitting instructions for both cartridge and cassette stereo tape players are the same, and in general the same rules apply as when fitting a radio. Tape players are not usually prone to electrical interference like radios — although it can occur — so positioning is not so critical. If possible the player should be mounted on an even keel. Also it must be possible for a driver wearing a seat belt to reach the unit in order to change, or turn over, tapes.

Radio interference suppression

Books have been written on the subject, so we're not going to be able to tell you a lot in this small space. To reduce the possibility of your radio picking up unwanted interference, an in-line choke should be fitted in the feed wire and the set itself must be earthed really securely. The next step is to start connecting capacitors to reduce the amount of interference being generated by the different circuits

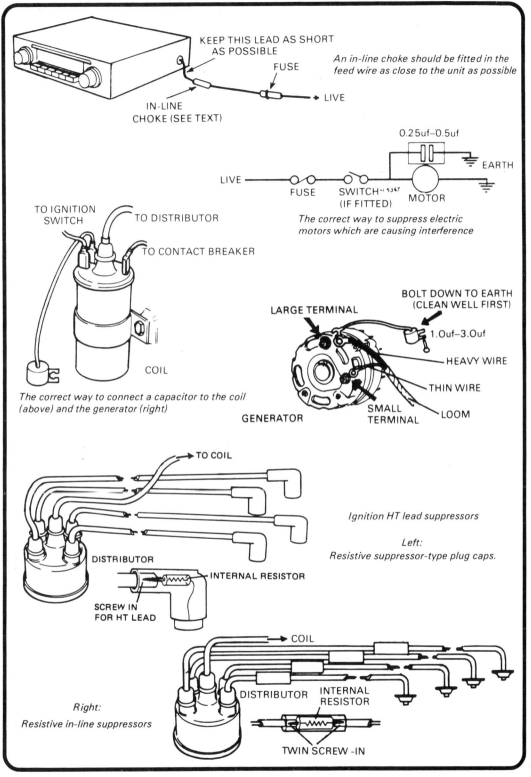

KEEP THIS LEAD AS SHORT AS POSSIBLE

FUSE

An in-line choke should be fitted in the feed wire as close to the unit as possible

IN-LINE CHOKE (SEE TEXT)

LIVE

0.25uf–0.5uf

EARTH

LIVE

FUSE

SWITCH (IF FITTED)

MOTOR

The correct way to suppress electric motors which are causing interference

TO IGNITION SWITCH

TO DISTRIBUTOR

TO CONTACT BREAKER

COIL

BOLT DOWN TO EARTH (CLEAN WELL FIRST)

LARGE TERMINAL

1.0uf–3.0uf

HEAVY WIRE

THIN WIRE

LOOM

The correct way to connect a capacitor to the coil (above) and the generator (right)

GENERATOR

SMALL TERMINAL

TO COIL

Ignition HT lead suppressors

Left:
Resistive suppressor-type plug caps.

DISTRIBUTOR

INTERNAL RESISTOR

SCREW IN FOR HT LEAD

COIL

DISTRIBUTOR

INTERNAL RESISTOR

Right:
Resistive in-line suppressors

TWIN SCREW -IN

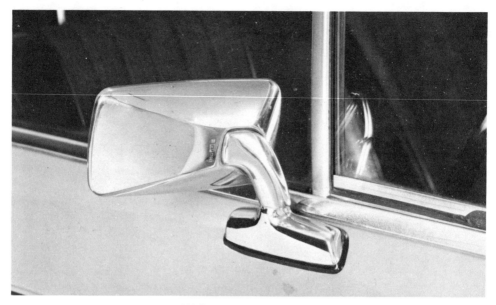

MAG 'European' door mirror

of the car's electrics. The accompanying illustrations show the various interference generators and give capacitor values for the suppressors. When it comes to the ignition HT leads, these are resistors which can either be suppressor-type plug caps or in-line suppressors; if you're already using resistive HT leads (those with the carbon fibre filling), they're already doing the job for you.

Visibility aids

Wing and door mirros

Recent EEC legislation has done wonders for the looks of exterior mirrors. In addition to being functional, they must now have no projections to catch clothing or other cars, and must fold flat when struck. The result is a new wave of products in all shapes and sizes, some of which can be sprayed to match up with the existing car finish. There's also been a marked swing recently from wing mirrors to the door-mounted kind, fitted as standard to some models.

Choose mirrors which you think will suit the car's styling and, having got them, select the mounting point carefully. You'll get a good idea of where the best place is by simply looking at other cars, but get someone to hold the mirror while you sit in the driving seat just to make sure you can see all you need to.

When fitting mirrors you'll first need to mark the hole position; then do likewise for the other side. Some door mirrors have a bolt type fixing, which will

mean removing the door trim panel; others are simply attached by self-tapping screws. For the larger holes, check the size needed and, if you can, select a drill this size plus, where applicable, a smaller one to make a pilot hole. If you haven't got a large enough drill, you'll have to drill one or more smaller holes and file out to the correct size. Don't forget to remove any burrs from the hole afterwards, then apply a little primer to cover the bare metal edges. When the primer's dry you can fit the mirror following the makers' instructions, then swivel it to get the best rear view.

For mirrors which only need self-tapping screws, make sure the drill used for the holes isn't too big. Ideally it should be fractionally larger than the thread root diameter – it's better to make sure that the hole's on the small side and enlarge it if necessary, rather than start off with a hole that's too big for the screws to bite properly.

Rear window demisters

At one time, if your car wasn't fitted with a heated rear window as standard equipment (and only the expensive models were), about the only remedy was a stick-on clear panel designed to act a bit like double glazing. They didn't usually work very well and frequently came unstuck too. Now they've been more or less superseded by the element type of stick-on demister. These act more like the genuine article, consisting of a metal foil element which is peeled off a backing sheet and stuck on the inside surface of the rear window glass. It has to be wired up to the electrical system, of course, via a suitable fuse and switch, using sufficiently heavy cable and preferably incorporating a warning lamp as it will take quite a large current and shouldn't be left on inadvertently. The great thing about these devices is that they do work, and are very moderately priced.

Headlamp conversions

Still on the subject of better visibility, if your problem's seeing in the dark then you might well consider uprating your headlamps. A number of conversions and more powerful bulbs are available, and mostly they're fitted by simply interchanging with the old ones, no wiring modifications being needed. If you're the owner of a 6 volt Beetle it's worth considering fitting a Quartz Halogen conversion kit to uprate your headlamps.

Comfort

Sound reducing kits

Longer journeys can be more pleasant if your car's comfortable to drive, and a couple of suggestions on this theme may be welcome.

Very few cars have yet been produced in which the noise level, particularly at motorway speeds, is all that could be desired. For economy reasons, most manufacturers put only a certain amount of underfelt and sound-deadening material into their cars, and a further improvement can usually be made by fitting one of the proprietary kits. These are usually tailored to fit individual models, and consist of sections of felt-like material which are glued in place under carpets, inside hollow sections, boot lid, etc, in accordance with instructions. The material can also be bought in rolls for D-I-Y cutting, using the carpets etc as templates.

Seats

If your seats are showing signs of old age (and new covers won't disguise the sagging, when you sit in them) then you can of course have them rebuilt by an upholstery specialist. On the other hand, you could think about replacing at least the driver's seat by one of the special bucket-types available. To look at these you'll need to find an accessory shop stocking the more motor sport orientated kind of goods.

Miscellaneous

Electronic ignition

Such systems are many and varied and most are widely advertised. The makers claim easier starting, better performance and lower fuel consumption as the main advantages, and on the whole these claims are substantiated in practice. However, before buying one of these kits we suggest you stop and consider whether your mileage and type of driving make the expenditure worthwhile. Get other advice, preferably from someone who's fitted such a system to his own car. Consider, too, whether you're capable of installing it yourself, otherwise you'll have to pay for fitting as well.

There are several types of electronic ignition – some retain the conventional contact-breaker in the car's distributor while others replace this by a magnetic triggering device. Even where the contact points are retained they're no longer likely to burn and therefore shouldn't need renewing very frequently – but this doesn't in itself amount to much of a saving.

Roof racks

Many an owner has to resort to a roof rack from time to time, even if it's only for family holidays. The types available are very varied, but they normally rely on clips attached to the water drain channel above the doors. If you're buying, select a size that suits your requirements (make sure that it's not too wide for the roof!) and don't overload it.

When fitting the roof rack, position it squarely on the roof, preferably towards the front rather than the rear. After it's loaded, by the way, recheck the tension of the attachment bracket screws. Don't keep the roof rack on when it's not wanted; it offers too much wind resistance and creates a surprising amount of noise (see *Save It!*).

Wide wheels

With increasing petrol and insurance costs, and decreasing speed limits, many motorists have stopped trying to get the ultimate in performance from a given engine size and drifted towards other things. One of these things, which not only smartens up the car but can also improve roadholding considerably, is a set of wide wheels.

You can get steel wide wheels which are less than half the price of a new radial tyre, but most people prefer the look of the light alloy ones. Practically all popular types are made from LM25 aluminium alloy; prices vary, but they'll certainly cost you more than the tyre that goes with them. For anyone who really wants to spend some money (and there can't really be any justification for it for normal road use) there are the magnesium alloy types; these'll set you back about twice as much as the aluminium alloy ones. You can even get steel wire-spoked wheels.

There was a time when all light alloy wheels had a bad reputation, but this seems to have improved considerably with the more modern casting **87**

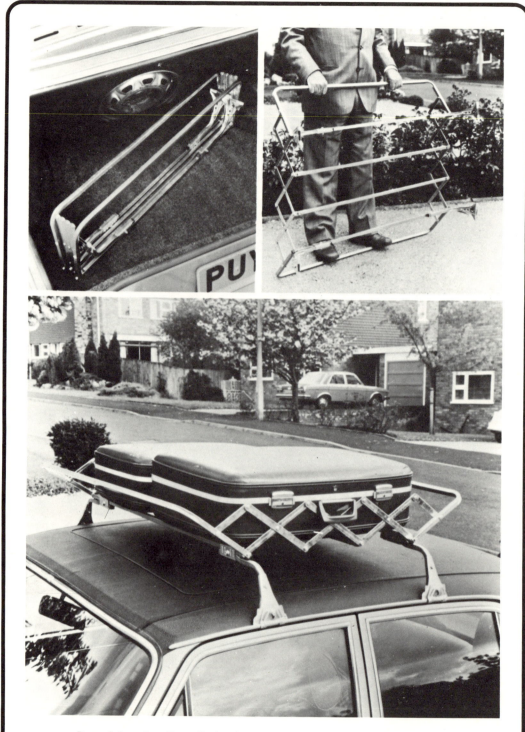

Desmo's ingenious 'Accordion' roof rack folds up to fit in the boot when not in use

techniques. They can still be porous, which could mean that you'll need a tube with the tyre if you're going to keep the air in, but they're normally sealed during manufacture to help overcome this. The wheels need to be treated with a little more care than steel wheels. To prevent corrosion setting in, it's important to keep them clean, particularly if there's salt on the roads, and to relacquer them from time to time. Don't drive into kerbs; a steel wheel might only suffer a dented rim but you can easily knock a piece out of a light alloy rim and that's the end of it.

When you're having tyres fitted, extra care must be taken to prevent the rim being damaged, and it won't do any harm to remind the tyre fitter at the time. Any balancing weights must be the stick-on type, not the ordinary clip-round-the-rim kind. The tyres themselves must be suitable for the rims, and because there are so many types around you'll have to take some advice from the wheel and tyre supplier.

One last point – flashy wheels are worth something on the thieves' market too, so it's worthwhile investing in lockable wheel nuts if your car's likely to be left unattended in lonely car parks for any length of time.

Steering wheels

One of the more popular, easily fitted accessories is a special steering wheel. Many types are available but often it's also necessary to buy a boss which fits onto the steering column shaft to accommodate the new steering wheel. No problems should be encountered when fitting a steering wheel or boss, once the old steering wheel has been taken off.

To do this, first disconnect the battery earth lead. With the front wheels in the straight-ahead position and the direction indicator lever in neutral, carefully prise the horn cap or pad assembly from the steering wheel. Disconnect the horn switch wire then unscrew the retaining nut and remove the washer. Pull off the steering wheel together with the horn ring, making sure it doesn't come off suddenly and hit you in the face (if it's stubborn refit the nut by a couple of threads and carefully thump the wheel from behind until it's free).

When you've finally remove the original steering wheel, you can commence fitting the new one. It's always better, if possible, to bolt the new steering wheel to the boss before attempting to slide the boss on to the steering column splines. When you're satisfied that the steering wheel and road wheels are pointing straight ahead, refit the washer and tighten the retaining nut. On later models you'll also have to refit the central plug.

Don't thump the steering wheel when refitting to models with a collapsible steering column or you may damage the inner column. In case you're interested,

the correct torque setting for the steering wheel nut is 5·0 kgf m (36·0 lbf ft). After you've tightened it, reconnect the horn switch wire and press on the cap or pad assembly.

Air horns

Air horns are marketed by several companies as a D-I-Y installation kit comprising the horns themselves, a compressor unit, a relay, plastic piping and electrical cable. What you've obviously got to do is mount the horns reasonably near the compressor, and the compressor reasonably near the relay, or the connections just won't reach. It's normal for the manufacturers to specify a certain way up for the compressor to be mounted, but there shouldn't be any other problems. You'll need to make sure that the electrical connections are as per the maker's instructions for the relay and compressor, and decide whether you want to use the air horns in conjunction with, or in place of, the original car horn. If you have to connect into existing wiring, make sure that the connections are well made and, if these involve soldering, don't forget to insulate any soldered joints.

Child safety seats and harnesses

A lot has been said and written in recent years about the use of seat belts for front seat passengers,

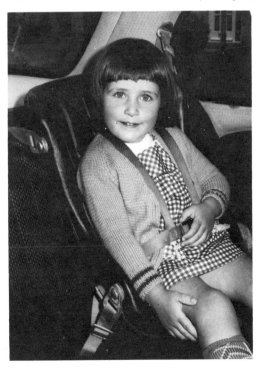

KL's 'Jeenay' child safety seat

The two later types of steering wheel

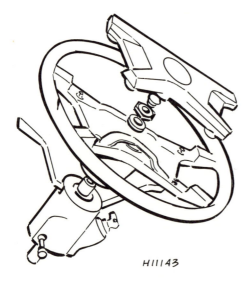
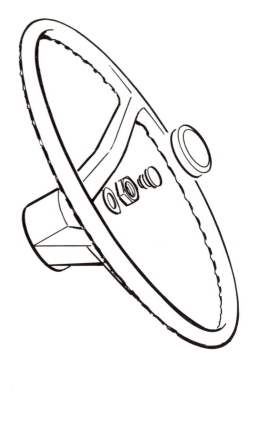

H11143

and more recently there's been an increasing interest in the various special rear seats and harnesses now available for young children. It's very difficult to give any precise instructions for fitting these, because there are so many types around, but what you must be careful about is ensuring that you buy a BSI-approved type.

Most types have a pair of straps at the front edge which need to be attached to the rear seat pan at the back of the squab, and a further pair of straps that fit over the back of the car seat for attachment to the rear floor or wheel arch. Take very careful note of the manufacturer's instructions; they require the anchorages to be a certain distance apart, and will probably also require reinforcing plates to be used. Before starting to drill holes for the mountings, make sure the underside or rear of the panel's clear of obstruction, pipes or any other components.

Mudflaps

90 You're probably already aware that both front and

rear wheel arches can be fitted with mudflaps. These will not only protect your car's underside and paintwork from flying stones, but will also earn the thanks of following drivers owing to the reduction in spray during wet weather. Fitting's straightforward and is usually by means of clamping brackets and screws.

Specialist fitments

We've now covered most of the main items likely to interest the average owner from the DIY fitting angle. Such things as towbars and sunshine or vinyl roofs, while practicable or desirable, are beyond the scope both of this book and of the ordinary car owner. We therefore recommend that for any major accessory of this kind you consult the appropriate specialist who'll be able to give an estimate of the cost, as well as carrying out the work properly and safely.

Troubleshooting

We've gone to great lengths in this book to provide as much information on your car as we think necessary for satisfactory running and servicing. Hopefully, you won't need to use this Chapter but there's always a possibility (rather than a probability!) that something will go wrong, and by reference to the charts that follow you should be able to pinpoint the trouble even if you can't actually fix it yourself.

The charts are broken down into the main systems of the car, and where there's a fairly straight-forward remedy — the sort you can tackle yourself — **bold type** is used to highlight it. Further information on that particular item will normally be found elsewhere in the book; look up the particular component or system in the index to find the correct page. In some cases a reference number will be found (eg T1/1); by looking up this number in the accompanying cross-reference table, you'll find more information on that particular fault.

TROUBLESHOOTER 1:

Starter motor doesn't work when key is turned

Starter motor doesn't work properly

Flat battery (T1/1).
Battery connec-
tions loose or
corroded.
Loose connection
to starter (T1/2).
Automatic
transmission
selector not at 'N'.

Starter motor or
solenoid switch
faulty internally

Doesn't turn engine

Starter pinion
jammed or not
engaging (T1/3).

Turns engine very
slowly

Battery flat or
defective (T1/1).
Internal starter
motor fault.

Spark plug lead(s)
loose, discon-
nected, or damp
(T1/4).
Spark plugs dirty,
cracked or
incorrectly
gapped.
Distributor or coil
cap damp, cracked
or HT lead loose.
Worn distributor
cap electrodes.
Coil or condenser
faulty (T1/5).
Contact breaker
points dirty or
incorrectly set.
Ignition timing
incorrect.

ENGINE — STARTING

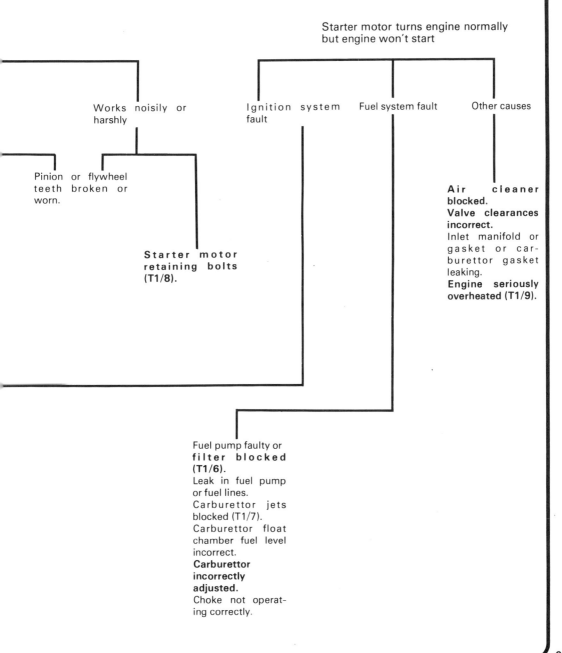

Starter motor turns engine normally but engine won't start

Works noisily or harshly

Ignition system fault

Fuel system fault

Other causes

Pinion or flywheel teeth broken or worn.

Starter motor retaining bolts (T1/8).

Air cleaner blocked.
Valve clearances incorrect.
Inlet manifold or gasket or carburettor gasket leaking.
Engine seriously overheated (T1/9).

Fuel pump faulty or **filter blocked (T1/6).**
Leak in fuel pump or fuel lines.
Carburettor jets blocked (T1/7).
Carburettor float chamber fuel level incorrect.
Carburettor incorrectly adjusted.
Choke not operating correctly.

TROUBLESHOOTER 2:

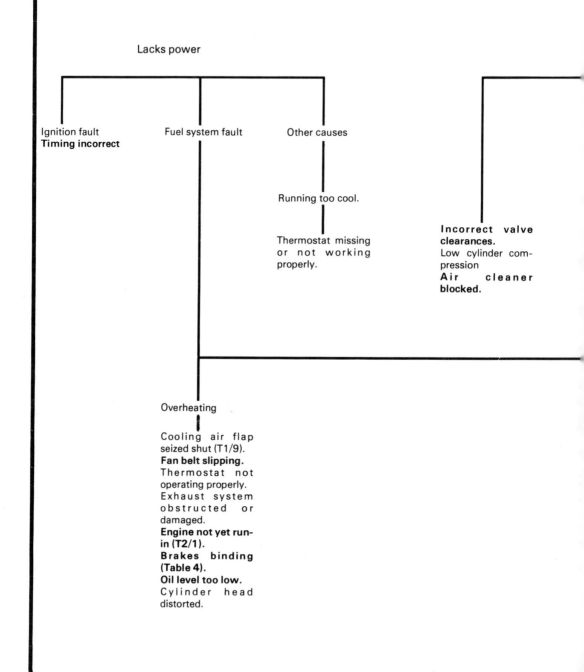

Lacks power

Ignition fault
Timing incorrect

Fuel system fault

Other causes

Running too cool.

Thermostat missing
or not working
properly.

**Incorrect valve
clearances.**
Low cylinder com-
pression
**Air cleaner
blocked.**

Overheating

Cooling air flap
seized shut (T1/9).
Fan belt slipping.
Thermostat not
operating properly.
Exhaust system
obstructed or
damaged.
**Engine not yet run-
in (T2/1).**
**Brakes binding
(Table 4).**
Oil level too low.
Cylinder head
distorted.

ENGINE — RUNNING

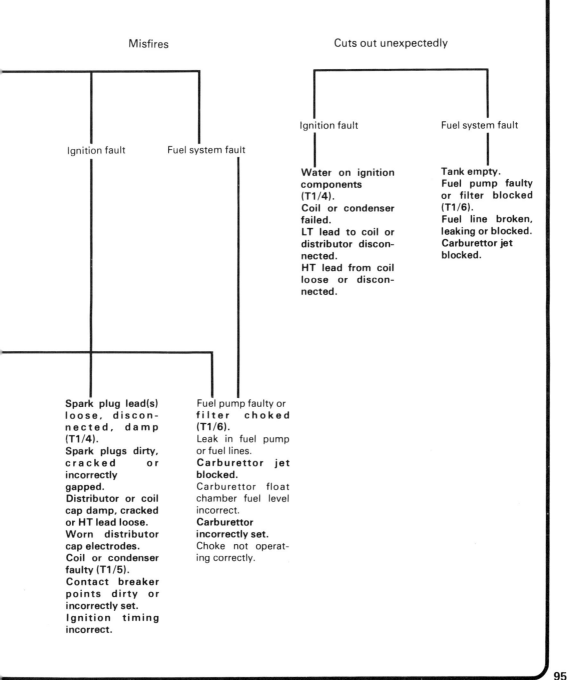

Misfires

Cuts out unexpectedly

Ignition fault

Fuel system fault

Ignition fault

Fuel system fault

Water on ignition components (T1/4). Coil or condenser failed. **LT lead to coil or distributor disconnected. HT lead from coil loose or disconnected.**

Tank empty. Fuel pump faulty or filter blocked (T1/6). Fuel line broken, leaking or blocked. Carburettor jet blocked.

Spark plug lead(s) loose, disconnected, damp (T1/4). Spark plugs dirty, cracked or incorrectly gapped. Distributor or coil cap damp, cracked or HT lead loose. Worn distributor cap electrodes. Coil or condenser faulty (T1/5). Contact breaker points dirty or incorrectly set. Ignition timing incorrect.

Fuel pump faulty or filter choked (T1/6). Leak in fuel pump or fuel lines. **Carburettor jet blocked.** Carburettor float chamber fuel level incorrect. **Carburettor incorrectly set.** Choke not operating correctly.

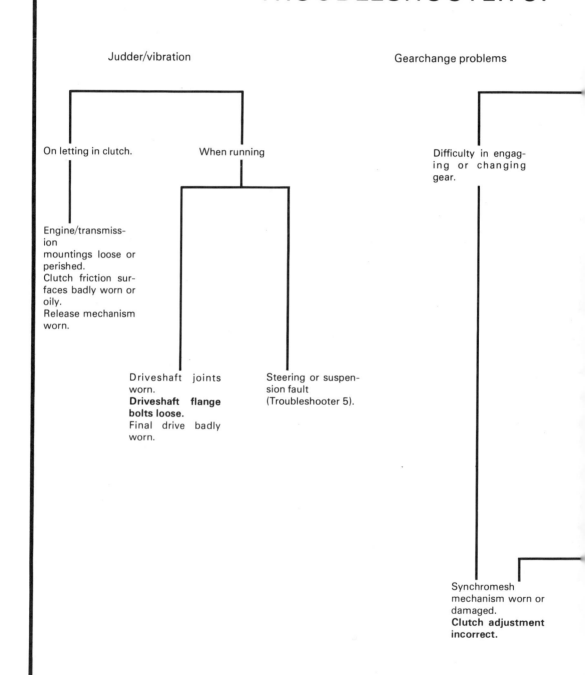

TROUBLESHOOTER 3:

Judder/vibration

Gearchange problems

On letting in clutch.

When running

Difficulty in engag-
ing or changing
gear.

Engine/transmiss-
ion
mountings loose or
perished.
Clutch friction sur-
faces badly worn or
oily.
Release mechanism
worn.

Driveshaft joints
worn.
**Driveshaft flange
bolts loose.**
Final drive badly
worn.

Steering or suspen-
sion fault
(Troubleshooter 5).

Synchromesh
mechanism worn or
damaged.
**Clutch adjustment
incorrect.**

CLUTCH & TRANSMISSION

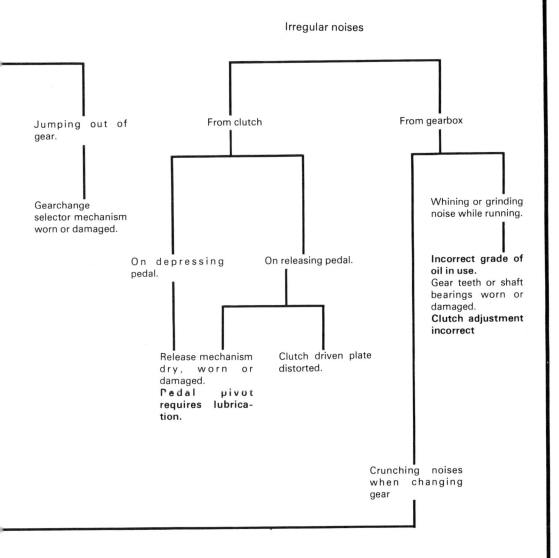

Irregular noises

Jumping out of gear.

Gearchange selector mechanism worn or damaged.

From clutch

On depressing pedal.

On releasing pedal.

Release mechanism dry, worn or damaged. **Pedal pivot requires lubrication.**

Clutch driven plate distorted.

From gearbox

Whining or grinding noise while running.

Incorrect grade of oil in use. Gear teeth or shaft bearings worn or damaged. **Clutch adjustment incorrect**

Crunching noises when changing gear

TROUBLESHOOTER 4:

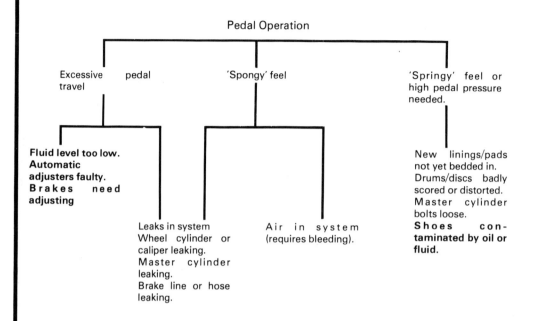

Pedal Operation

Excessive pedal travel

'Spongy' feel

'Springy' feel or high pedal pressure needed.

**Fluid level too low.
Automatic
adjusters faulty.
Brakes need
adjusting**

New linings/pads not yet bedded in. Drums/discs badly scored or distorted. Master cylinder bolts loose. **Shoes contaminated by oil or fluid.**

Leaks in system Wheel cylinder or caliper leaking. Master cylinder leaking. Brake line or hose leaking.

Air in system (requires bleeding).

TROUBLESHOOTER 5:

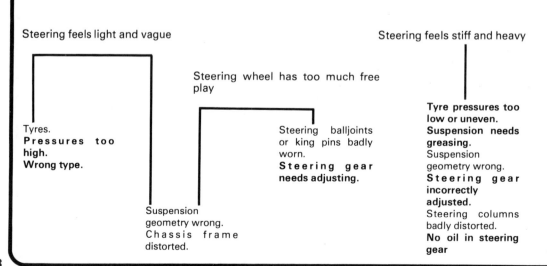

Steering feels light and vague

Steering feels stiff and heavy

Steering wheel has too much free play

Tyres.
**Pressures too
high.
Wrong type.**

Steering balljoints or king pins badly worn. **Steering gear needs adjusting.**

**Tyre pressures too
low or uneven.
Suspension needs
greasing.**
Suspension geometry wrong. **Steering gear incorrectly adjusted.** Steering columns badly distorted. **No oil in steering gear**

Suspension geometry wrong. Chassis frame distorted.

BRAKES

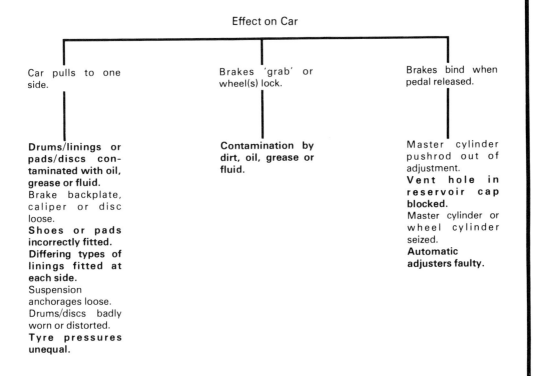

Effect on Car

Car pulls to one side.

Drums/linings or pads/discs con-taminated with oil, grease or fluid.
Brake backplate, caliper or disc loose.
Shoes or pads incorrectly fitted.
Differing types of linings fitted at each side.
Suspension anchorages loose.
Drums/discs badly worn or distorted.
Tyre pressures unequal.

Brakes 'grab' or wheel(s) lock.

Contamination by dirt, oil, grease or fluid.

Brakes bind when pedal released.

Master cylinder pushrod out of adjustment.
Vent hole in reservoir cap blocked.
Master cylinder or wheel cylinder seized.
Automatic adjusters faulty.

STEERING AND SUSPENSION

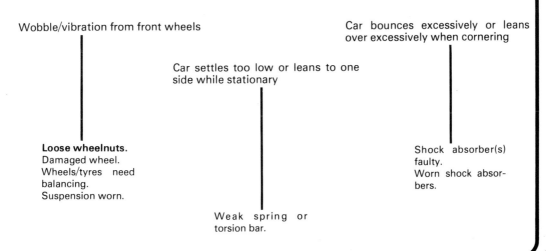

Wobble/vibration from front wheels

Loose wheelnuts.
Damaged wheel.
Wheels/tyres need balancing.
Suspension worn.

Car settles too low or leans to one side while stationary

Weak spring or torsion bar.

Car bounces excessively or leans over excessively when cornering

Shock absorber(s) faulty.
Worn shock absor-bers.

TROUBLESHOOTER 6:

Note: This chart assumes that the battery installed in your car is in good condition and of the correct specification, and that the terminal connections are clean and tight. A car used frequently for stop-start motoring or for short journeys, (particularly during the winter when lights, heater blower etc are likely to be in use) may need its battery recharged at intervals to keep it serviceable. If an electrical problem occurs, don't immediately suspect the starter or any other component without first checking that the battery's capable of supplying its demands!

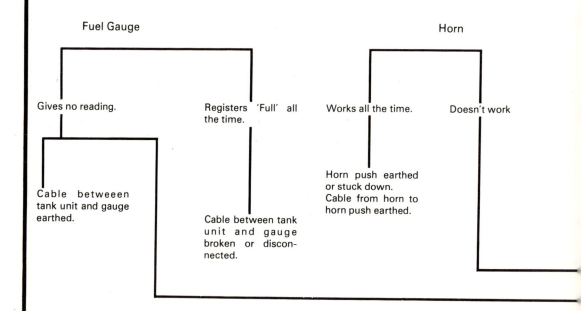

Fuel Gauge

Gives no reading.

Registers 'Full' all the time.

Cable betweeen tank unit and gauge earthed.

Cable between tank unit and gauge broken or disconnected.

Horn

Works all the time.

Doesn't work

Horn push earthed or stuck down.
Cable from horn to horn push earthed.

ELECTRICS

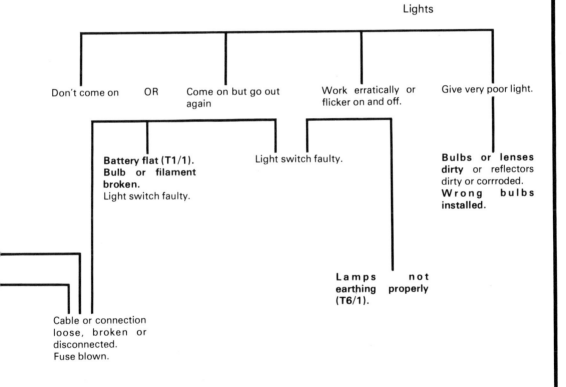

Lights

Don't come on   OR   Come on but go out again   Work erratically or flicker on and off.   Give very poor light.

**Battery flat (T1/1).
Bulb or filament
broken.**
Light switch faulty.

Light switch faulty.

**Bulbs or lenses
dirty** or reflectors
dirty or corrroded.
**Wrong bulbs
installed.**

Cable or connection
loose, broken or
disconnected.
Fuse blown.

**Lamps not
earthing
(T6/1).**

A fault occurring in any other electrical equipment or accessory not specifically referred to can usually be traced to one of three main causes, ie blown fuse; loose or broken connection to power supply or earth; or internal fault in the component concerned.

CROSS-REFERENCE TABLE

TROUBLESHOOTER REFERENCE	ADDITIONAL INFORMATION
T1/1	Either charge the battery from a battery charger, or use jumper leads to start the car from another battery; make sure that the lead polarities are correct in both cases or you may do permanent damage, particularly if your car has an alternator.
T1/2	If the lead's loose, disconnect the battery earth lead then tighten the connection on the starter motor. Reconnect the battery earth lead.
T1/3	If the starter pinion's not turning, it's probably jammed in mesh with the flywheel teeth; try engaging top gear and rock the car to and fro to free it.
T1/4	Make sure all the connections are tight, then wipe the leads clean and dry with a lint-free cloth. Use an ignition system waterproofer (eg WD40 or Damp Start) to prevent problems in the future.
T1/5	An ignition coil is a simple item to fit, but make a note of the connections before removing them, and ensure that the replacement coil is the correct type. To remove the condenser if it's fitted inside the distributor, first remove the contact points. If it's on the outside disconnect the wire.

TROUBLESHOOTER REFERENCE	ADDITIONAL INFORMATION
	Unscrew the retaining screw and withdraw the condenser.
T1/6	To check the operation of the pump, detach the fuel outlet pipe (that's the one that goes to the carburettor) and turn the engine on the starter motor. Take care you don't spill fuel on a hot exhaust. Cleaning the fuel pump filter is covered in the 3000 mile Service Schedule.
T1/7	Unscrew the jets from the sides of the carburettor and blow them clear before refitting them.
T1/8	Not very easy to get at but with a small spanner it is possible without removing other items.
T1/9	Make sure that the fan belt's adjusted correctly and that the thermostat is not holding the cooling air flap shut. Also check the oil level.
T2/1	Drive slowly!
T6/1	Remove the lamp lens where necessary (see *In an Emergency*) and trace the earth wire to the chassis. Disconnect the wire and remake the earth by scraping any rust away.

CONVERSION FACTORS

Distance

Inches (in)	X 25.400	=	Millimetres (mm)
Feet (ft)	X 0.305	=	Metres (m)
Miles	X 1.609	=	Kilometres (km)
Millimetres (mm)	X 0.039	=	Inches (in)
Metres (m)	X 3.281	=	Feet (ft)
Kilometres (km)	X 0.621	=	Miles

Capacity

Inches, cubic (cu in/in³)	X 16.387	=	Centimetres, cubic (cc/cm³)
Fluid ounce, imperial (fl oz)	X 35.51	=	Centimetres, cubic (cc/cm³)
Fluid ounce, US (fl oz)	X 29.57	=	Centimetres, cubic (cc/cm³)
Pints, imperial (imp pt)	X 0.568	=	Litres (L)
Quarts, imperial (imp qt)	X 1.1365	=	Litres (L)
Quarts, imperial (imp qt)	X 1.201	=	Quart, US (US qt)
Quarts, US (US qt)	X 0.9463	=	Litres (L)
Quarts, US (US qt)	X 0.8326	=	Quarts, imperial (imp qt)
Gallons, imperial (imp gal)	X 4.546	=	Litres (L)
Gallons, imperial (imp gal)	X 1.201	=	Gallons, US (US gal)
Gallons, US (US gal)	X 3.7853	=	Litres (L)
Gallons, US (US gal)	X 0.8326	=	Gallons, imperial (imp gal)
Centimetres, cubic (cc/cm³)	X 0.061	=	Inches, cubic (cu in/in³)
Centimetres, cubic (cc/cm³)	X 0.02816	=	Fluid ounces, imperial (fl oz)
Centimeters, cubic (cc/cm³)	X 0.03381	=	Fluid ounces, US (fl oz)
Litres (L)	X 28.16	=	Fluid ounces, imperial (fl oz)
Litres (L)	X 33.81	=	Fluid ounces, US (fl oz)
Litres (L)	X 1.760	=	Pints, imperial (imp pt)
Litres (L)	X 0.8799	=	Quarts, imperial (imp qt)
Litres (L)	X 1.0567	=	Quarts, US (US qt)
Litres (L)	X 0.220	=	Gallons, imperial (imp gal)
Litres (L)	X 0.264	=	Gallons, US (US gal)

Pressure

Pounds/sq in (psi/lb/sq in/lb/in²)	X 0.070	=	Kilogrammes/sq cm (kg/sq cm)
Pounds/sq in (psi/lb/sq in/lb/in²)	X 0.068	=	Atmospheres (atm)
Kilogrammes sq cm (kg/sq cm)	X 14.223	=	Pounds/sq in (psi/lb/sq in/lb/in²)
Atmospheres (atm)	X 14.696	=	Pounds/sq in (psi/lb/sq in/lb/in²)

Torque

Pound - inches (lbf in)	X 0.0115	=	Kilogramme - metres (kgf m)
Pound - inches (lbf in)	X 0.0833	=	Pound - feet (lbf ft)
Pound - feet (lbf ft)	X 12	=	Pound - inches (lbf in)
Pound - feet (lbf ft)	X 0.138	=	Kilogramme - metres (kgf m)
Pound - feet (lbf ft)	X 1.356	=	Newton - metres (Nm)
Kilogramme - metres (kgf m)	X 86.796	=	Pound - inches (lbf in)
Kilogramme - metres (kgf m)	X 7.233	=	Pound - feet (lbf ft)
Newton - metres (Nm)	X. 0.738	=	Pound - feet (lbf ft)
Newton - metres (Nm)	X 0.102	=	Kilogramme - metres (kgf m)

Speed

Miles - hour (mph)	X 1.609	=	Kilometres - hour (kph)
Feet - second	X 0.305	=	Metres - second (m/s)
Kilometres - hour (kph)	X 0.621	=	Miles - hour (mph)
Metres - second (m/s)	X 3.281	=	Feet - second
Metres - second (m/s)	X 3.600	=	Kilometres - hour (kph)

Index

**Printed by
Haynes Publishing Group
Sparkford Yeovil Somerset
England**